Acclaim for *Code Name: God*

"*Code Name: God* develops in such a way that readers are won over wholeheartedly by Bhaumik's convictions. The metaphors and analogies used in *Code Name: God* appropriately balance its scientific tone and add extra beauty to its reader-friendly style. Although Bhaumik's goal is to bridge the gap between modern physics, spirituality, and cosmology, an inquisitive reader will see several bridges in the book linking science, literature, art, philosophy, and life."
— *Science and Theology News*

"This book may change your life."
— Sidney Sheldon, best-selling author

"The author's personal odyssey from a life of abject poverty in Bengal to one of excessive luxury in Hollywood, from ancient Indian wisdom to advanced laser physics, and finally back to his roots in the attempt to find common ground between Eastern spirituality and Western science is eloquently told and makes for fascinating reading."
— Fritjof Capra, author of the international bestseller *The Tao of Physics*

"Mani Bhaumik offers us his scientific genius in order to present a compelling new argument for mysticism and faith. His conclusions are rich, vivid, and contemporary;

his propositions honestly and generously put forth. This book is a gift to the world and a powerful story beautifully told." — Paula D'Arcy, author of *Sacred Threshold* and *A New Set of Eyes*

"The merging of matter and spirit, as presented in this book, might facilitate a much needed evolutionary step forward in our capacity to love and be fair."
— Laura (Mrs. Aldous) Huxley, founder of Children: Our Ultimate Investment

"A fascinating story. The book is a serious read but the results for the reader will be worth the effort. Dr. Bhaumik's Eastern religious perspective is as applicable to the science/religion argument as that of many Western writers. Recommended for most libraries."
— *Catholic Library World*

"A fascinating account of the author's journey from a life of abject poverty in an Indian village, to excessive opulence as a millionaire on the Pacific Coast, and then to the realization he was spiritually bankrupt. His journey back to faith is through his work in laser physics. A must-read for any man or woman of science seeking God."
— *The Poetry Church*

code name: GOD

THE SPIRITUAL ODYSSEY
OF A MAN OF SCIENCE

MANI BHAUMIK

A Crossroad Book
The Crossroad Publishing Company
New York

The Crossroad Publishing Company

Printed in the United States of America

This text of this book is set in 11/15.5 Korinna.
The display face is Calligraphic 421.

Bhaumik, Mani.

    Code name God : the spiritual odyssey of a man of science / Mani Bhaumik.
      p. cm.
    Includes bibliographical references.
    ISBN 0-8245-2281-8; ISBN 0-8245-2517-5 (pbk)
    1. Bhaumik, Mani. 2. Religion and science. 3. Spiritual biography – India. 4. Spiritual biography – United States. I. Title.
    BL73.B475A3 2005
    204'.092 – dc22

                          2005001598

ISBN 13: 978-0-8245-2517-0

To
Seekers of Truth
of All Times

Science without religion is lame,
religion without science is blind.

Albert Einstein

Contents

Prologue

The Wound That Must Be Healed

IMAGINE THAT the mind of man and the mind of God comprise an exquisitely designed broadcast system. It operates on a single channel. Suppose also that the universal mind transmits at a frequency that is omnipresent, but can be picked up only by a receiver tuned to operate in resonance with it. As with all radios, static must be eliminated to get a clear signal. Our wondrous brains ought to be up to the task. But could there be a problem? Have we perhaps forgotten the location of the channel on our radio dial? Have we even concluded that the station, after many years, has gone off the air?

On April 8, 1966, *Time* magazine, an oracle of American opinion, asked, in boldfaced red, "Is God Dead?" But the world did not come to a grinding halt, for this cover story had been centuries in the making.

The belief in a divine power dominated world thought until about four hundred years ago, when scientific discoveries and philosophical skepticism began to shake our faith in what we could not see, sift, or quantify. Following René Descartes' rigid division between mind and matter, pioneers of early science developed empirical knowledge without reference to God or the human mind. By the nine-teenth century, Karl Marx, whose ideas would significantly influence the history of the following century, was dis-missing religion as the opiate of the masses, and Charles Darwin's *The Origin of the Species* discounted the Biblical story of creation.

After Friedrich Nietzsche's proclamation that God is dead, humankind seemed to sink into a slough of despair, sometimes bordering on panic, since we were fearful that we had lost all sense of direction. Sigmund Freud, the fa-ther of modern psychology, urged people to regard God as an illusion, nothing more. He said our concept of God only symbolized an infantile desire for a father figure, and we should outgrow this desire. Science should replace God, Freud decreed, explaining: "Science is not an illu-sion. But it would be an illusion to suppose that we could get anywhere else what it cannot give us."

But science also proved to be a false god, and its world-view left many despondent, among them even the atheis-tic philosopher Jean-Paul Sartre, who wrote of "the God-shaped hole in the human head" through which the Cre-ator had been forcibly extracted. From the mind-matter dualism of Descartes to the iconoclasm of Nietzsche and Marx, from the existentialism of Sartre to the counterfeit reality of the *Matrix* movies, the split between man and maker has long been widening, and many acknowledged that the wedge was Science with a capital "S." Specifi-cally, classical physics, with its mechanistic view of the cosmos, had cut God from man's psyche, leaving in its postoperative haste an open wound of spiritual despair, tyranny, and endless war.

The truth is, both spirituality and science are essential to human beings and always have been. Strangely enough, the same scientific method that once compelled us to question the existence of God is now, by way of advanced physics and cosmology, developing evidence that tends to support our age-old belief in a transcendent power.

A sea change has occurred, though many readers of *Time* may not have oriented themselves yet to a quan tum universe: where the same tiny particle may occupy two places at one time or react instantly to events light years away; where the net energy of the cosmos is zero, yet there is more energy in the vacuum of space than in all the stars; where physics is close to proving that material reality emerges from a common source, which I'll refer to as the *primary field*. Is this the field where God has been at play all along? Can humankind tune in God's frequency once again? I believe we can, in part by means of our own quantum leap in consciousness.

The ideas and observations I offer in the following pages surely cannot span the measure of that leap, for your own full participation is essential. Perhaps, though, my story will encourage you to take a further step on life's greatest journey. (If you are reading this book, you've already embarked!)

This is the memoir of my quest for a new kind of faith. It is a faith in which mind and matter entwine, yet it is anchored in the empirical precepts of science. It is a belief system that says directed consciousness can promote

spontaneous remission of a life-threatening disease, a personal quantum leap. It embraces a worldview wherein
quantum leaps do occur, not just in the atomic and subatomic domain but in human existence itself—be it in the
unfolding of an individual life, in a societal change, or in a
country's struggle for freedom.

I will not ask you to accept that view "on faith." Let me
offer a proof of it by way of my own life, starting at the point
when I was the least certain of its meaning and value.

I

After the Ball

FROM THE BEGINNING, there was a touch of unreality about my life in the fast lane. I am a scientist, not a celebrity, and the scientist in me is forever asking, "What's wrong with this picture?"

The balcony of my home in Bel Air, California, faced the Pacific, and from it I could see Catalina Island, miles offshore. Its golden hills were haloed by the setting sun; its mythically named port of Avalon teased me — a self-made millionaire — just as the green light on Daisy Buchanan's pier had taunted Jay Gatsby, reminding him that in spite of his accomplishments, he would never truly belong to her world.

As I looked on, the island might suddenly vanish from the horizon like a trick of the light, and sadness would envelop me as thickly as a coastal fog. Was my wealth likewise illusory? Were the trappings of my success as ephemeral as that distant island seemed to be? And if not, why did I want more? Why wasn't I satisfied? After all, I had come to America from a place where a man with a roof over his head and a cow might well be the richest man in town. Could it be that I had left something behind?

In the early stage of this spiritual crisis, when I doubted the reality of my fortune, I could stroll the perimeter of my Olympic-sized pool, watch the videotape of my turn on *Lifestyles of the Rich and Famous,* or hop into my Rolls-Royce and visit one of five other houses I'd built with the bounty of my work in laser technology. And if that inventory failed to reassure me, I could look forward to the evening's gala, when once again my driveway would fill with the limousines of the celebrities and moguls whose company I was now entitled to keep. The presence in my home of titled aristocrats and trendsetters seemed empirical proof of the fact that I had escaped the horror and hopelessness of my childhood and would live happily ever after.

Before long, however, even the prospect of Château Lafite Rothschild and beluga caviar, of witty conversation and glamorous women, and of the affirmation of status that all of this provided failed to dispel either the monotony of going from excitement to excitement or the gnawing sense of having lost my way. One hears often of spiritual rebirth arising from despair and destitution, but as in the examples of St. Francis, St. Augustine, and the Buddha, it can also be prompted by an *absence* of want, a compulsive consumption — a queasy feeling of being overfed and undernourished at the same time. The result — if it is not substance abuse or mental illness — can be a profound and pervasive discontent, a sense of letdown succinctly expressed in Peggy Lee's classic ballad, "Is That All There Is?"

My Peggy Lee moment arrived, if such things can be pinpointed, on a breezy night following yet another soiree at my Bel Air estate. The limousines had departed, the caterers had packed up, and I was alone beside the swimming pool, the faint sounds of other parties — far too many to attend them all — echoing in the deep, leafy canyon. A place card rustled past my feet, nudged by the wind. I looked down and saw that it bore the name of a famous guest. I don't recall who it was, only that it suddenly did not matter.

Curiously, I found myself staring at my shoes, good Italian leather. They were barely worn, and they might not be worn again. After all, I had a closetful. But once upon a time I had walked the rice fields of Bengal, India, barefoot, the smell and the texture of shoe leather as foreign to me as foie gras. I didn't own my first pair of shoes until I turned sixteen.

In those days, though my stomach ached from hunger and my pulse throbbed with the anxiety of an uncertain tomorrow, I never walked alone. All around me in the damp, infested night, embedded in the very fabric of the perfumed darkness, was the undeniable presence of that living web from which all things are born and continually unfold. That presence, which the Vedic *rishis* called Brahman, and that Lao-tzu called the Tao; He that the prophets of the Book called Yahweh or Allah, and that later in my own life I would come to call the *one source*. At once, I knew the cause of my unhappiness.

That presence was missing.

The darkness, on that night in Los Angeles, held no such all-pervading presence. And since what is truly ageless and unchanging can never simply go *poof,* the cause of its absence, I realized, must be an emptiness within me.

In the language of theology, this peculiar kind of sadness is called a "loss of faith"; some trauma or disillusionment has shaken our belief that something holds everything together. I had made my way in the world as a scientist, supposedly immune to such spiritual desolation. Was I really immune? I believe no one truly is. Oddly enough, it was as a scientist that I'd once glimpsed evidence of a cosmic unity that is beyond blind faith. Could I find such unity again?

From the days of my boyhood in India, from the example of my father and my grandmother and, especially, of the great Mohandas K. Gandhi, I had learned that faith must always be underwritten by action. I was also fortunate enough to observe Mother Teresa epitomize faith in action with her unwavering dedication to helping the poorest of the poor in Calcutta.

I stooped to pick up the stray place card, along with champagne corks, cocktail napkins, and other detritus of that night's urgent merriment, and dropped them into the trash. Then I resolved that I would pledge myself to working in concert with others of a common desire to forge a new alloy of spirituality and science, one strong enough — even in its web-like delicacy — to withstand the centrifugal forces of our age.

However many (or few) houses I was destined to own in the future, I did not want to feel again so completely alone in them. However many lovely islands I might be privileged to gaze at, I wanted to know that both their worldly reality and their evanescent magic had unfolded from the same source that had shaped my own being.

Mani's mansion in Bel Air, California.

2

Great Expectations

JUST AS A REFUGEE, separated from his homeland for many years, can begin to forget his native tongue, or a prisoner, denied human contact, loses his social skills, I had become estranged from both my knowledge of advanced physics and my spiritual roots. I had in many ways become a prisoner of my worldly success.

My mind, that had gotten me from Bengal to Bel Air, was now calibrated for quick wit and congeniality, not for contemplation. It was out of shape, and so was my spirit. We tend to forget that mind and spirit, though abstract, are as essential to our fitness as a strong heart, and they demand their daily workouts no less. I set about to relearn as a mature man, with a scientist's desire for proof, what I had once known intuitively.

This, I quickly discovered, is a goal easier to set than to accomplish, for the mind hardens as arteries do. How to limber it up? When we find ourselves in the wrong place, it is instructive to look at how we got there, even to backtrack and try to retrieve some of what we've lost along the way. Only this process of looking back and seeing forward, of existing fully in the present while connected to both past and future, can make us complete.

And so I began by surveying the distance I had traveled and the people and forces that had shaped me en route to my lonely mansion on the hill.

I was not an overnight success. The jackpot that my colleagues and I at the Northrop Corporation hit in 1973, with the first conclusive demonstration of the excimer laser, didn't come until I'd been in America for fourteen years. I had worked my way from a wide-eyed immigrant to a middle-class householder, and finally to a degree of financial autonomy and confidence that at long last had allowed me to step from the shadows of low self-esteem and social insecurity.

A Sloan Foundation Fellowship and the sponsorship of UCLA's Professor William McMillan had opened the door for me to America and its promise of prosperity. My work in advanced physics as a post-doctoral fellow at UCLA built upon my Ph.D. dissertation at IIT, India's equivalent of MIT. Based on my studies in electronic energy transfer, in 1961 I was added to the research team at Xerox's Electro-Optical Systems, where I became a champion of the chelate liquid laser and experienced my first taste of financial reward. In 1968, I was brought into Northrop's corporate laboratories and subsequently promoted to manager of laser technology.

We will speak later of laser light and its analogy to certain spiritual states. For now, it is sufficient to say that the excimer laser for which I'm known found one of its primary applications in corneal sculpting, the type of corrective eye surgery made popular by LASIK.

The accomplishments that vaulted me into the ranks of America's so-called rich and famous came, however, only after prior decades of scrambling — sometimes with little foothold — up from the dark well of my childhood.

My story properly begins in the impoverished region of east India where I was born and raised. In retrospect, it seems I began my struggle to escape its cycle of despair from the moment I fought my way through the birth canal onto the mud floor of my family's hut. I would have preferred to begin life on cool marble or thickly woven carpets, but despite its poverty there were treasures to be found in the hamlet of my birth. India is a living contradiction. Jewels may well be concealed in the cloaks of beggars.

My village was located near the ancient Buddhist port of Tamluk, not far from where the Bengal tigers roam. My father, Gunadhar Bhaumik, was a schoolteacher whose day job concealed his true passion: the liberation of India from the iron grip of the British colonial Raj. He was a stern, distant man, but his idealism and his devotion to Gandhi's non-violent revolution made him a valued foot soldier. Unfortunately for me, it also frequently made him an absent father.

My mother, Lolita, was a simple village woman, bound to my father at the age of eleven by the time-honored agencies of family connection, marriage brokers, and astrologers who declared the stars aligned for a successful union. The marriage was not consummated until she came of age. In accordance with custom, a second marriage was held before they were allowed to share a bed. Thus was my somewhat unpromising entrance on the stage of life delayed by a few years.

My paternal grandmother, Sarada, was the true center of the family. She was a reed-thin woman with snowy hair, and I will always hear her kind words and Bengali lullabies in concert with the rustle of her white linen sari. In Indian tradition, it was to her that my young mother deferred in matters of my upbringing, and, in truth, my mother had little choice if she wanted to remain under our roof.

Sarada spoiled me, but what child living on a relief agency diet does not deserve a little spoiling? She often shared her food and sweets with me, and some years later, at the point of our greatest peril, she would, in this way, teach me that great love is more verb than noun.

Yes, we were poor, often close to starvation, but so were most of our neighbors. I had been born to a place that seemed to vacuum all energy. A lolling, blank-eyed resignation afflicted everyone I knew. Yet this was India, and even in the midst of squalor, the aromatic bouquet of spirituality rose from the ground like morning vapors. The omnipresence of God was a fact of life.

The everyday rapture of Indian village life, underpinned by both daily ritual and by the great *pujas,* or festivals, fostered a communitarian spirit that leavened our despair. To earn the respect of one's fellow human was the primary social aim. To feel unity with God, of whom we were told we were all a part, was the supreme spiritual goal. Most

people believed such an experience of oneness was beyond their grasp, and they left these spiritual leaps to the
"experts" — the *rishis* and seers — deriving a sort of sec-
ondhand ecstasy from ceremony and music. My parents,
though faithful to their daily devotions, were of this more
modest spiritual ambition.

There are times, however, when India casts her spell on
even the reluctant mystic, giving the aspiring seeker (at
the unripe age of ten) reason to continue his quest. One
such time occurred in the fall of 1941.

On a moonless night, my father and I were walking
home from the local bazaar along a muddy path bordering an irrigation canal that fed water to the rice paddies. I
was barefoot. The darkness was near total, for there was
no electricity in the villages and we could not afford the
oil for a lantern. A fragrant breeze rippled the rice paddies
with little waves, which I took for watery phantoms, but in
spite of the presence of ghosts, I felt safe in my father's
company.

Though small and slender, my father was a man of great
inner strength and an intensity ferocious enough to rival
any Bengal tiger's. He had, a decade before, given his
body and soul to Gandhi's freedom movement and was
constantly under suspicion by the colonial authorities. Because the police would not have hesitated to threaten his
family, my father's visits home were sporadic and, for me,
incalculably precious.

It may have been the security of his presence that allowed me the serenity to become suddenly and profoundly
aware of the world around me. The night songs of frogs

and crickets rose to a full chorus, filling the silences between us. My father was sparing with words and displays
of affection. Perhaps he feared that emotional intimacy
would only deepen his family's grief should he die at the
hands of the Raj, or maybe a life of risk had taught him
that listening is a dearer survival skill than talking.

Although his remoteness made my heart ache, it also
drew me out of myself. A raven rose from the paddies,
disturbed by our passage. As I followed the beating of its
wings upward, I beheld the sky as never before, and my
heart opened to receive it.

The stars, I knew, had always been there, but on this
night their infinitude overwhelmed me and flooded my
consciousness with an indescribable feeling of unity. They
formed an endless canopy across the black velvet heavens, so vast as to be beyond any grasp and yet seemingly
close enough for a small boy's reach.

At that age, I understood none of the awesome forces
that had brought this spectacle into existence. I knew
nothing of scientists like Bohr or Bohm and hardly more
of the nature of Brahman, our name for the Architect of
the Universe. A barefoot village boy like myself could
point out the Big Dipper and perhaps tell something of the
devas, or local deities, but until this night, the bigger picture had been beyond me. I saw that my father, too, had
paused beside me to gaze in amazement at the stars and
that his silence was somehow both deeper and less distant
than usual. In a moment of trust and kinship, I asked him,
"Father, is this God?"

For an instant, I thought he might affirm my suspicions. I could see that he was moved. But the question, coming from a ten-year-old, took him by surprise. A disconcerted look crossed his face, as if he were searching for an answer suitable to a small boy pondering such a big question. "It's none of your business," is what he came up with, probably hoping to dam up a river of questions he perhaps could not answer.

Needless to say, his reply did not satisfy me, though I now understand that my father's mind and heart were attuned to more immediate concerns, like the suffering of his neighbors and his own survival, and not to the great mysteries of the cosmos. "I wouldn't worry my head about these things," he continued. "You're too young. Maybe some day you will learn all there is to know about the world and its wonders, but for now, do not seek to delve into them or analyze them. It is enough that you revere them."

My father was wrong, but only in the way that all fathers are wrong when they seek to defer their children's hard questions, and that all practical men are wrong when they separate heaven from earth or mind from matter. A saying is attributed to the mythical Egyptian teacher, Hermes Trismegistus: "As above, so below." In light of the revelations of modern science, we now know that the same force of gravity that made the apple fall on Newton's head also keeps the entire cosmos together, and that the natural laws we discover here on earth apply throughout the universe. We might also say, "As little, so big"; the unimaginably vast universe emerged from an infinitesimal subatomic dimension. Science no longer allows us to sever heaven from earth or mind from matter.

The question I asked my father was to be the first of many, for from that moment on, I did think and wonder — and delve into and analyze — every physical phenomenon I encountered, posing the same query in a thousand different ways. What I experienced on that night, only vaguely knowing it, was my first intoxicating taste of both scientific and spiritual insight, but it was not to be the last.

My grandmother, Sarada, was in many ways the emotional opposite of my father. While he was rooted in hard social and political reality by a revolutionary's fervor to alter it, she never failed to open my eyes to the golden light at play behind even the darkest of circumstances.

One day, she took me to a tributary of the sacred Ganges River, about a three mile walk from our village. Together, we climbed a high embankment, and as I bent to catch my breath, I saw glimmering before us the vast expanse of water. The river was so wide and swollen by rain at this point that the far bank was beyond the horizon; as far as I knew, the river went on forever.

Once again, I felt the vastness before my eyes shift my awareness to another level altogether, to the sphere that I learned later in life was that of genuine mystical experience. It was as if the consciousness of nature interpenetrated my own and found itself at home there.

What were these experiences, "scientifically speaking"? Why did they make me feel the way they did? In years to come, I would learn that the essence of consciousness pervades the universe and that our brains may well be designed to tune into it and receive as much as we can, providing we are able to surrender the space.

I refer not to the individualized ego-consciousness, but to that cosmic consciousness which Vedic seers of my native land called Brahman.

If this sounds like pure metaphysics, the words of Max Planck, godfather of quantum theory, may be instructive: "I regard consciousness as *primary*. I regard matter as *derivative* of consciousness" (my italics). And from Sir Arthur Eddington, the renowned physicist and astronomer: "All through the physical world runs that unknown content that must surely be the stuff of our own consciousness."

Looking back to India from where I am now, across the blue Pacific, beyond Australia, beyond Southeast Asia, to a small village in the humblest part of the sub-continent, I know that the map of my life was changed beside the whispering rice paddies and on the muddy banks of the Ganges. I cannot say with certainty that the success I enjoyed later is in any way the result of these shifts in my boyhood perceptions, but I am certain that both our triumphs and our tragedies are defined as much by *how we perceive* as by *what we do,* another lesson that I have taken pains to relearn.

It is a long road from my primitive birthplace to the landscaped hills of Bel Air. On the face of it, no two environments could be less alike, yet I have realized that they have at least one element in common: my consciousness. I took no greater care with the fine floors in my Los Angeles home than my grandmother Sarada did with the mud floor of our hut. Each morning she wiped it down with a moist cloth as if it were the rarest marble, and what pride she took in it! I was born on that floor, and I would like to close this chapter by telling that story.

I was delivered as the sun was setting, and there was no breeze. The women of my village gathered around, as they had for ages, to assist my mother through her labor. I am told that I arrived quickly and without much difficulty (anxious as I must have been to begin my escape!), but there was one complication: the existence of the caste system in India.

The task of cutting the umbilical cord was considered so unpleasant that only the bottom rung "untouchables" were deemed lowly enough to perform it. The problem was that, at that moment, there were no untouchables in the neighborhood. And so there I lay, alternately listless and kicking on the cool mud, bound to my young mother until the break of dawn, when my father was at last able to locate an old woman who used a sharp piece of bamboo skin to sever the cord. The long night, during which custom required that my mother remain seated upright, caused damage to her uterus that brought great pain and prevented further conception for another ten years.

But a different scenario is imaginable: We might both have died right there on the kitchen floor. Still, no one would have dared cut the cord. The irony is that my family was merely one rung higher on the Hindu social ladder than the humble untouchable who freed me to embark on my journey. If there is an anecdote that more simply illustrates the self-defeating foolishness of the social and

religious barriers we erect against one another, I do not
know of it.

If this little tale were the heart of my experience in
India, I might choose to spare further details. On the contrary, what separates people in India is overpoweringly
surmounted by what joins them. And it is of this oneness that I wish to speak next, for it is at the core of
both mysticism and the boldest advances in modern physics. I offer as support for this linkage the fact that Erwin
Schrödinger and Werner Heisenberg, pioneers of quantum
physics, both embraced the mystical in their mature years.
A true science does not favor substance over spirit, but
recognizes each in the other.

3

One from Many, Many from One

IF YOU WERE TO STAND in my village today, the emerald green of the boundless rice paddies reflected in each teardrop of morning dew, you would see it almost exactly as I did. Very little has changed in the furnace of modernity. Although in the cities the caste system has withered — due to Gandhi's transformative influence — to little more than a social pecking order, its influence abides in the hinterlands, as do the customs, colors, and crushing poverty of my youth.

Should you decide to linger near the place where I was born on a balmy autumn night during the *Durga Puja,* our counterpart to Yuletide festivals in the West, you would still smell sandalwood and clove incense and the tempting sweetness of *sandesh,* the seasonal treat, a ricotta-like curd flavored with sap extracted from date palms. The same intoxicating music would fill the air, and, above all, the voices would be raised in the same chants of praise to Durga, the mythical deity who vanquished evil in the form of the buffalo demon, Mahisasura.

Other *pujas* and rituals filled other seasons and flavored nearly every slice of time: months, weeks, days, hours. The Kali Puja, which followed Durga's, celebrated the chaotic power of that feminine dynamo with the fearsome face, Kali's upside-down morality embracing the destructive forces of nature. The local *bamun,* or priests, presided over the rites of Laksmi, goddess of wealth, each Thursday. Swaraswati, goddess of learning, was honored regularly in our household. And every night, as the women prepared for their evening devotions, the oil lamp was lit and the conch shell blown to bring a soft curtain down on the day.

So much ritual, so many gods and demi-gods, and yet Hinduism, that kaleidoscope of related belief systems that once defined Asia, is at its core no less monotheistic than Judaism, Christianity, or Islam. Those who study the Vedas, the foundational teachings of Indian spirituality, know that all deities are but manifestations of a single godhead, Brahman, and that Brahman is itself — like the fabric of the universe — undivided, unchanging, and all-pervading. It is from India and from the Vedas in particular that the world first learned the notion that God is One. All separateness, including the separateness of our own selves, simply disguises the underlying unity of things.

This sense of cosmic kinship — that in India seems to permeate the weave of every fabric, the aroma of each simmering curry, the air itself — is expressed succinctly by the Vedic credo: *Aham Brahmasmi.* I am Brahman. The belief that each one of us completes creation and that, correspondingly, God is incomplete *without us,* is at the root of Indian life and may, along with the concepts of karma and maya, help explain why Indians are able to endure hardship with a certain equanimity. But is this belief really different from that expressed in the statement attributed to Jesus Christ by the Evangelist John: "I and the Father are one"?

The Vedic sense of Brahman as being more like a ubiquitous force field than the persona of a distant and all-powerful cosmic ruler is strikingly close to the Western theological concept of immanence, that holds that God's spirit pervades the universe, and, most importantly, that he lives in us. For centuries in the West, notwithstanding Jesus' assertion that "the Kingdom of Heaven is within," an openly stated belief in immanence could bring a man or woman dangerously close to heresy, but then so could an assertion that Earth orbited the sun. The latter belief challenged the primacy of Earth in the celestial order, while immanence challenged the primacy of the church in the terrestrial order. As above, so below!

It was finally science that established the truth of a heliocentric solar system (and it must be acknowledged that many early Western scientists were also devout Catholics). It may also be science that, in our age, provides a theoretical foundation for the reality of immanence and — not without a certain irony — puts God back on the cover of *Time,* albeit without the traditional white beard.

It will, indeed, be a very different picture of God from the one most of us hold in our minds. It is difficult to say at this point how the cover artist might conceive God. Based on the revelations of modern science, it seems a good bet that the picture will bear some resemblance to what the great *rishis* of the Vedic tradition have seen and experienced in their deepest meditations, for modern science tells us that the whole of the universe is flooded by a sea of energy — a clear light, if you like — that fills what is known as the quantum vacuum. It is a light so pervasive that we would, in truth, only be able to "see it" if it were not there. It is the first created thing, like the "Let there be light" of Genesis, but it is still not the first thing. The entity that created it, the Brahman of both science and spirit, is an even more wondrous and perplexing thing to contemplate, for it is a single point and it is all points.

When we later discuss the correlations of modern science and ancient wisdom in greater depth, we will learn, for example, that the quantum field theory of particle physics postulates that fundamental particles, like electrons, are absolutely identical whenever or wherever they come into being in the universe because they are, in actuality, ripples in the same pervasive sea — excitations of the electron field that permeates the whole universe. This relates to the idea that events in one sector of the universe are linked to events in another, that everything is, at the deepest quantum level, everywhere. That all is one. Thus, science moves ever closer to saying that we are made of the stuff of God, and that any other perception is what the great Rig-Veda calls maya: illusion.

One might be tempted to crow that the *rishis* of three or four millennia past were eons ahead of Planck, Einstein, and Roger Penrose, or even that religion had beat science to the punch, but the truth, as always, is more complicated, for we must always take into account the human propensity to miss the forest for the trees.

Not far from my birthplace, in the remote Khasi Hills of the northeast, the tribal kings known as the *syiems* still perform annually their single royal function of behead-ing two dozen sacrificial goats, each one of which must be killed with a single stroke if the king is to retain his office and his dignity. Each year in Benares, thousands flock to bathe in the sacred waters of the Ganges, one of the world's most polluted rivers. In relatively cosmopoli-tan New Delhi, well-educated people propitiate the demon god Bhairon with rum and vodka, seeking to insure health or a good return on their investments. And in my little village, young married women, desperate to conceive so as not to disgrace their husbands may still cling to the necks of milk cows, as my mother Lolita did, begging to be blessed with the gift of fertility.

So India presents a paradox. It is profound and prim-itive, deeply spiritual and darkly superstitious, both uni-versalistic and maddeningly provincial, with an ethical system that places community well above the individual and yet allows outrages like the caste system and the often murderous rivalry of Hindus and Muslims. In many ways, the land of my birth is — like my adopted country of Amer-ica — a mirror of human society's best and worst, and though the two countries reflect these extremes differently, they have much in common.

Both India and America endured British imperialism for nearly two centuries, and both eventually threw off

the yoke in revolutions based on the ideal of equal treatment under the law. Both nations have been great "melting
pots," accommodating a staggering variety of races, na-
tionalities, and belief systems, yet each has also been
stained by intolerance and social prejudice. Both have
survived brutal schisms that might have destroyed lesser
nations.

America has emerged from these trials rich and forward-
thinking yet predominantly materialistic and spiritually
ambivalent. India is still plagued by poverty and strife, yet
remains spiritually vibrant and perhaps more in sync with
the abstract realities described by modern science. It has
often occurred to me that each country could use a taste
of the other's medicine.

My parents were devout Hindus, disciples of the great
nineteenth-century guru Ramakrishna, who was himself a
devotee of Kali. Every morning and evening, my mother
retired to an area of the hut set aside for *Aradhana* — the
daily rituals and offerings of her faith. There, she medi-
tated in an atmosphere redolent of incense, flowers and
flickering candlelight, a faded photograph of the deceased
guru before her. (It is a common misperception in the West
that the faithful actually see the gilt-framed photos and
statuettes of Hindu worship as gods, when in fact they
serve more as focusing tools for the discipline of meditation; it is easier for most people to relate to a holy man
or an icon than it is to the abstraction of Brahman.)

As little else could be done while devotions were in
progress, I remember sometimes creeping up to watch
my young mother in her quietly ecstatic embrace of the

divine. My grandmother, never far from my side, both encouraged my interest and admonished me not to disturb
my mother. I had no idea what she was doing, chanting
mantras in a language no one spoke and appearing utterly
removed from the world outside our hut. In that world, children suffered for want of a cup of broth and colonial police
enforced the rule of the Raj with iron-fisted brutality. Yet
here was my mother, blissed out despite it all.

Years later, when as a college boy I undertook to learn
the ancient art of meditation, I came to see that my
mother, through her simple ritual, was able, twice each
day, to purchase a brief respite from the hardship of her
life, and thus was more able to bear it. Many anxious and
over-stressed Americans of today would doubtless benefit
from such a time out.

My father practiced meditation as well, though separately, and there was poignancy in my parents' *Aradhana;*
they desired spiritual unity with God, but believed this was
unattainable within the normal stream of life. Only total
renunciation of material existence and retreat to the Himalayas or some other spiritual outpost would bring them
their heart's desire, and this was, of course, impractical.
I have come to believe that it is possible to achieve enlightenment without leaving the world behind, but not by
rejecting the persuasion of my ancestors. On the contrary: I believe, like Gandhi, in putting faith into action and
exploring it no less than we explore the nature of the atom.

In the beginning, my interest in Indian religion did not
extend beyond the epic folklore of the *Ramayana* and
the *Mahabharata,* the Hindu equivalents of the *Iliad* and

the *Odyssey*. But as my fascination with modern science grew, so did my desire to comprehend its mythical and spiritual antecedents.

Written in ancient Sanskrit, the four Vedas and their subsequent elaboration in the Upanishads were humankind's first recorded spiritual thoughts. In one of the most influential messages in the Upanishads, we are counseled: "Taking as a bow the great weapon of Upanishad, one should put upon it an arrow sharpened by meditation. Stretching the bowstring with a thought directed to the essence of being, penetrate the imperishable as the mark." Following such advice, for centuries Indian mystics were able to bring their minds, through meditation, to a state of sublime alertness and awareness.

It is notable that neither such exercises nor such metaphors were restricted to the "mystical East." They find parallels in the writings, for example, of the anonymous fourteenth-century monk who wrote *The Cloud of Unknowing,* and who advises, "Pay careful heed, then, to this exercise, and to the wonderful way in which it works within your soul. For when rightly understood, it is nothing else than a sudden impulse, one that comes without warning, speedily flying up to God *as the spark flies up from the burning coal.*" Similar thought is to be found in the works of St. John of the Cross, Meister Eckhart, the Kabbalist Isaac Luria, and the Sufi al-Ghazali. Meditation and true prayer are both practiced with the intent of dissolving into God.

We learn in another Hindu text, the Bhagavad Gita, that our chaotic thoughts, swarming with a multiplicity of

facts, ambitions and obsessions, are only disjointed frag-
ments of one basic reality, Brahman. "Kill therefore with
the sword of wisdom the doubt born of ignorance that lies
in thy heart," says the Gita. "Be one in self-harmony, in
Yoga, and arise, great warrior, arise." To be "in yoga" is
to be yoked with Brahman, the entity that transcends all
boundaries of self and object. Again, from the Gita: "Brahman, without beginning, supreme: beyond what is and
beyond what is not."

The Upanishads are unequivocal about the essential
oneness of God: "People say, 'Worship this god! Worship
that god!' But this is all Brahman's creation! He himself
is all gods." The Rig-Veda, an astonishingly ancient com-
pendium of hymns, mantras, and instructions for properly
articulating them, tells us that Brahman used the magical
"veiling power" known as maya to create the universe we
see and experience, and that karma is the dynamic force
of necessity that keeps everything "in action."

We will see that this notion is not so very different from
the scientific principles of the universal fields, such as
electromagnetism, that stabilize the swarm of subatomic
particles of which any object is made into a "material"
form. If a chair is a chair, it is because forces are acting
upon its molecules, its atoms, in order to keep it as such.
But what is it really?

What is being alluded to by widely misunderstood catch
phrases such as "Nothing is real" or "All is illusion"? The
point is not to say that your dog, or your car, or your
spouse does not, in reality, exist. They exist, but only as
organized energy. Like Durga, Kali, Krishna, Shiva, and all

the myriad personages of the Indian repertory company, they are but embodiments of Brahman.

"All actions take place on the stage of time by the interweaving of the forces of Nature," says the Gita. "Only the man lost in selfish delusion thinks himself to be the actor. But the man who sees the relationships among these forces also sees how they act together to create the world."

This is the mystery of India. It is the riddle whispered in the ear of every child. I was later to learn that modern physics stood face to face with the same mystery, and it was moving toward the conclusion that some singular entity akin to Brahman enfolded all others.

But of what substance, of what numinous fabric is Brahman made? Even when I was a boy, India challenged me with this question. I vowed to answer it, but first I had to survive long enough to grow up.

4

Faith in Action

THEY CAME in the dead of night, demanding to know my father's whereabouts, their bayonets wiped clean and menacingly ready to spill more Indian blood. The colonial police who served the British Raj knew that our simple hut had become a gathering point in Tamluk for the revolutionary movement that simmered throughout the 1930s and boiled over in 1942, when millions of Indians demanded, along with their leader, Mohandas Gandhi, that the British "Quit India!" once and for all.

The police were never far behind my father, but it must have bedeviled them to enter our home and find that he had seemingly vanished, in the blink of an eye, into the vaporous atmosphere of Bengal. Though I believe I knew — even as a boy of eight or nine — that he could not make himself invisible, it often appeared so. In fact, he might have been no more than fifty yards away, hiding in plain sight, and herein lies a lesson not only in guerilla warfare but in physics and mysticism, as well. You cannot "locate" something that presents itself in a form you do not expect to see, even if it is right before your eyes.

On this night, as on many others, my father had slipped
into the hut while the village slept, a brief return home
in the midst of days — sometimes months — of life in
the revolutionary underground. He had left his job as a
schoolteacher to join Gandhi's freedom movement full-
time, leaving us admiring his dedication but without a
source of income. The combination of an empty belly and
a deep sense of abandonment stirred resentment in me,
and yet the sound of his voice, murmuring in concert with
my mother and grandmother as I lay curled at their feet,
was as welcome as rain after a drought. I knew he would
not stay for long, and his fleeting visits were burned into
my memory as moments both magical and laden with
dread, for in his wake, the police were bound to follow.

"Where has he gone?" the senior policeman demanded,
while his underlings ransacked our hut. "Tell us or you'll
regret it!" The question was met with stoical silence from
the two women, and as for me, I truly did not know. "Fine,
then," the officer said. "We are taking your eating uten-
sils away. You can eat off banana leaves like the peasants
you are. Do you really imagine that the likes of Gunadhar
Bhaumik will overthrow the mighty Raj?"

The officer approached me with his billy club raised.
"And you, you little wog. What do you have to tell us, eh?"
I can still remember the cold fear I felt and the acrid mix of
sweat and service cologne coming off his uniform. I shook
my head, and he raised the club higher.

"You cannot strike a child!" my grandmother protested.
"Hit me, if you must have blood." Her entreaty spared me
the policeman's billy club, but not the rage behind it. I got

the back of his hand instead, and as the blood poured from my nose, I collapsed to the floor with nothing before my eyes but stars.

My grandmother rushed to my side, knelt, and lifted my head from the ground, aiming a glare of contempt at the policeman equal to any words she might have uttered. My mother wept bitterly, for she was young and frightened, paralyzed by helplessness. The officer, sniffing her vulnerability as a shark senses blood in the water, raised her trembling chin with the end of his club.

"When you are ready to have your things back," he said to her, "just tell us what we want to know." He shook his head. "What kind of husband leaves a wife to fend for herself in a hellhole like this?" Then he stalked out, his lackeys following, their arms heaped with our only valuables. He turned once at the door to add, "If not, there will be more of the same."

I think that of the many crimes an authority figure may commit, whether he wears the outfit of a colonial occupier, a priest, or a prison guard, the worst is to make another feel powerless. I could not relieve my mother's anguish, but I resolved that I would find the tools to empower myself.

Eventually, those tools came to me from an unexpected source, a bounty that is available to all, and they consisted of neither guns nor political or economic might. Before this could happen, however, I had life lessons to learn, and for these lessons I am indebted to my grandmother Sarada, to Mohandas Karamchand Gandhi, and to an extraordinary woman by the name of Matangini Hazra.

It was on another of my father's clandestine visits that he brought into our home a poor, middle-aged widow whom he had inspired to join the movement in 1932. By the time I met Matangini, she had been working with him for some years. Her life was a model of faith, courage, and, moreover, perseverance. For lack of adequate dowry, she had been a bride at age twelve to a man of sixty, became a widow at eighteen, and then was driven into the streets by her own stepson. Few women in Bengal could have survived such a loss of status, yet she provided for herself by living in a shack and husking paddy. She was to become one of India's founding daughters, and she was both mentor and friend to a small, scrawny Bengali boy who had few of either.

For me, Matangini came to embody, in action and spirit, Gandhi's guiding doctrine of *Satyagraha,* that though loosely characterized as "soul force," he defined as "the vindication of truth not by the infliction of suffering on one's opponent, but on one's self." In other words, if one *wills* himself to endure even worse than what his enemy can dish out, there can be no victory over him.

To post-modern Western sensibilities, this may seem a kind of collective masochism, but in practice it led to massive civil disobedience and, at its peak, it brought the machinations of the British Raj to a grinding halt. It was a brilliant strategy, and one should not wonder why. A very similar sort of passive resistance and willful self-sacrifice essentially contributed to bringing down the Roman Empire. "The enemy," Gandhi said, "must be weaned from error by patience and sympathy."

Patience and sympathy were not, as one can imagine, qualities easily summoned by people like Matangini and my father, freedom fighters who longed to rid India of what Gandhi called the "curse" of British rule. They agreed with him that the Raj had "sapped the foundations of our culture" and "reduced us politically to serfdom," but the notion that such oppression could be overcome through patient toil and education was not an easy one to accept.

It might have been more natural for them to follow the path of Netaji Subhas Bose, a firebrand nationalist who advocated violent revolution and was Gandhi's chief rival for leadership of the movement. But Gandhi's impact on those who encountered him lit the fuse of revolution in their spirit, where no bayonet could penetrate. His lessons were always taught by example, and his command was always in the front line, which led U.S. Secretary of State George Marshall to call him "the spokesman for the conscience of mankind" and his fellow Indians to name him Mahatma: Great Soul. By the time I met his devotee Matangini Hazra, her soul had also been enlarged.

Matangini's love for Gandhi was so great that she became known in our village as *Gandhiburi,* the old Gandhian woman. Although I later had the good fortune to meet Gandhi and serve in his camp, it was through Matangini that I came to know his message and that my own spirit was infused. I drew courage from her story and from her practical idealism, and glimpsed for the first time that the exercise of active faith might yet make it possible for me to escape that primitive and hopeless place, where apathy and abject resignation to poverty hung in the air like a poison mist.

Above all else, Matangini taught me the virtue of tenacity. "Never give up," was her refrain, and I learned to repeat it almost as a mantra. "Nothing happens without a fight," I now understood to mean a struggle within as well as without, a fight against the crushing odds of anything truly wonderful ever occurring. Though she was uneducated, and deeply regretted it, she encouraged me in my studies and realized, perhaps even before my own family did, that I was different from other boys my age.

If the greatest evil that one can do is to make another person feel powerless, it may be that the greatest good is to empower: to recognize that spark of potential in the soul of another and to use one's own strength — even one's last breath — to fan it into flame. Matangini did this, and more; she taught me to live without fear because she herself was fearless.

Bengal province was a hotbed of anticolonial fervor, and Tamluk was its flashpoint, for wherever the disparity between power and powerlessness is greatest, there will the fire burn hottest. Wherever the chasm separating desire from its object is widest, there the most daring leaps will be made. "Blessed are they which do hunger and thirst after righteousness, for they shall be filled." One blazing afternoon, a freedom march was held in the district capital. Its destination was the palace of the governor, who stood supremely and insouciantly out of reach on his balcony, observing the march as if it were some curious native custom or perhaps a cricket match. Belying the governor's lack of concern was a phalanx of rifle-bearing guards, three men deep, which lined the street between the marchers and the palace.

Matangini marched in the parade's vanguard, holding the freedom movement's flag high. As they reached the point directly in front of the governor's balcony, she suddenly broke through the bayoneted cordon, brandishing her banner, and screamed, "Go back, *lat sahib!*" before the stunned soldiers could take her down. She was promptly arrested and sentenced to six months at hard labor, and upon her release — though haggard and malnourished — she went immediately to do social work among the untouchables, as Gandhi had instructed his followers to do. She was a force of nature, and I am convinced that she had tapped into the vital source that has been the object of my own quest.

Eventually, the colonial police caught up with my father, too, and he was imprisoned and tortured for his devotion to Gandhi's *Satyagraha,* a devotion that he refused to renounce. I cannot imagine how he suffered it, except to say that he had also surmounted fear. "Blessed are they which are persecuted for righteousness' sake, for theirs is the kingdom of heaven." And though there were hard days to go before the sun finally set on the British occupation of India, I can't help but think that the willful suffering endured by my father, Matangini, and countless others took its toll on their persecutors as well.

It may be asked why, in a book devoted to the union of science and spirituality, I am dwelling at length on India's suffering in her struggle for freedom. It is not simply because of a desire to tell my story, nor even my great wish to honor those whose souls have brushed mine and left it immeasurably richer. Perhaps my reason is best expressed this way: It is no less arduous a task for the mind to free itself of the illusion of subject-object separation (from nature, from one another, from God) than for a nation to free itself from a colonial oppressor. The genius of Mahatma Gandhi was to perceive that the two struggles are essentially one. "One must be the change one wishes to see in the world."

5

Faith in Action

A Year on the Brink

IN THE SUMMER of 1942, as soon as Gandhi embarked upon the Quit India campaign, the colonial government again imprisoned him. He launched a three-week personal fast that very nearly finished him.

The British, who no longer had the option of quietly executing the undeclared leader of India and couldn't risk the upheaval that would ensue if he starved to death on their watch, implored Gandhi to relent and leave the prison. Gandhiji, as we affectionately called him, would not budge until the next step toward self-rule was taken and, ultimately, he prevailed.

During a campaign that spanned more than three decades, Gandhi spent 2,089 days — a total of nearly six years — in Indian prisons, on top of the 249 days he previously had logged in South African jails. There was not a prison built that could contain his spirit, nor a torture devised in the darkest of hearts that could break his will.

Matangini Hazra was also a tiger for justice, and her service to the Quit India movement in Tamluk was decisive

and dramatic. Even amid the ferment of revolution, however, she never forgot me. One evening in the fall, when the
rains had abated, leaving the air clean and humid, Matangini came to our hut bearing a plate of *pithas* — Bengali
sweetmeats — which she had made for me, knowing that
it was one of my favorite treats. She sat at my side on our
mud floor and popped them one by one into my mouth,
as she had done when I was small.

"Gandhiji is in prison again," she said, in a grave but
steady voice.

I stopped chewing and looked at her. My eyes must have
betrayed my fear, for she put her hand on my arm and
nodded for me to eat.

"Nothing happens without self-sacrifice," she said.
"And, sometimes, death. But we must never give up, even
in the face of our own end."

She blessed me and reminded me that as long as my
actions were right, I need never be frightened of anyone or
anything. In spite of her reassurance, there was something
in her manner that alarmed me. I lay awake that night with
a dark apprehension, my stomach content but my heart
aching.

The next day, Matangini joined with thousands of un-
armed freedom fighters in a march to confront the colonial
guards at Tamluk. Like the civil rights workers in Selma,
Alabama, and the anti-war protestors of the 1960s, they
faced guns with only the shield of their conviction. Matangini carried the flag of Gandhi's movement and a conch
shell as her trumpet. Undeterred by what I am certain
were her own forebodings, she took up a position in the

front lines and shouted, "Bandemataram!" (Revere your Motherland!) as they approached the edgy soldiers, who must have feared karma almost as much as they feared the crowd's passion.

And it happened the way it always happens. One nervous young guard opened fire, and the others followed in a fusillade. The men flanking Matangini broke and fled, but she advanced steadily into the fire.

The first bullet tore through her left hand and her conch shell fell and shattered on the pavement. No matter. She wrapped her bloody fingers around the flagpole, having two hands now free to hold the flag all the higher. The second bullet lodged in her leg. Matangini stumbled and fell briefly to the ground before rising again, waving our colors like a torch and crying "Bandemataram!"

The third bullet entered her forehead and burst through the back of her skull, and though my beloved Matangini's soul had left her body, still she managed to walk another three steps before crumbling. Even so, the soldiers who surrounded her fallen body like scavengers feared what life remained within her, and they had to pry her fingers from the mast, lest the flag that continued to flutter on the gunpowder breeze exhort others to martyrdom.

Two weeks later, as if in Old Testament wrath against an India still not cleansed of the colonial curse, nature unleashed more misfortune on Bengal in the form of a killer cyclone. It struck in mid-October 1942, decimating entire villages and destroying the year's harvest, the only means of survival for a people who ate just what they could grow.

Hundreds died as trees across a wide swath of the province were uprooted and hurled into homes with hurricane force. As the flood waters rose steadily higher, my family was finally forced to clamber onto the roof of our hut, helpless to do anything but watch, wait, and pray for the waters to recede.

On the night we made our uncertain beds barely a foot above the rising water, I felt a horror I knew of only from my grandmother's stories and, until that night, had been no more real to me than the buffalo demon, Mahisasura. I will never forget the thunderous roar from all directions as an enormous tidal wave broke the shores of the Bay of Bengal and surged inland, sweeping away everything in its path. Many of our neighbors, their houses already gone, stood no more chance of surviving than the weakest of the animals.

Even though the waters rushed by, our simple roof held fast and so, somehow, did we. But what was left when the gray morning came made our survival somewhat moot. There was no food, neither in our village nor the neighboring villages; the reserves from the previous year's harvest had been consumed already. There was no one to come to our rescue, least of all the Raj, who must have seen our catastrophe as a divine reprieve for His Majesty's Empire. Surely it was only a matter of time before we all perished.

Although the high waters had receded, they left behind a veritable bayou, unsuitable for rice or any other crop. One day, as I was walking home, I leapt across what I thought was a swollen tree trunk, and cried out loud when it bobbed over to reveal a corpse — half-eaten by the dogs — of a boy like myself. This will be my fate, I thought, unless we could get to the cities. I had heard that there was food in the cities, and I could not understand why it was being denied to us. No child's mind is wired to comprehend a human capacity for cruelty on the scale exercised by the colonial rulers against the people of Bengal, not even a child who has seen his family repeatedly terrorized.

The plain fact was that we were being punished for our insurgency, for the unyielding pressure that men like my father had brought to bear on the Raj. I can almost hear the exchange, over a breakfast of eggs and kippers in the officers' mess: "What's to be done about Midnapore, sir?" The reply: "In Midnapore, nature will be permitted to take its course." The Bengal famine of 1943 was an act of social engineering, and if you survey the planet today with an unblinking eye, you will discover that most famine is due to politics, politics that disregards the hollow eyes of a starving child.

An Associated Press dispatch of December 10, 1943 — a full year after the cyclone had struck — read as follows: "In Midnapore, corpses are to be seen floating in the canals, prey to dogs and vultures. Within a quarter-mile of Tamluk town, we witnessed the body of a woman, recently deceased, being devoured by a strong, stout dog." Indeed, when hell is brought to earth, the dogs are more likely to survive than the people.

Disease follows opportunistically on the heels of disaster, and the cyclone's legacy of epidemic cholera and malaria, combined with the famine, killed three million of my countrymen. I would not be alive to tell you this but for the transcendent love — the faith in action — of one person.

What little food we could procure during the famine made, at best, for one meager serving per day, and even that would not have kept us all alive for more than a few weeks. My grandmother Sarada began to give her portions to me. She made no show of it and asked no acknowledgment. No one but me knew of her sacrifice. To conserve what scant energy she had, she retired after each meal to her blanket and stared listlessly at the light coming through the cracks in the door. I knelt by her side and clasped her bony hand, sharing in her secret plot to make one life from two.

For days at a time, Sarada ate hardly anything at all, and soon she fell ill from malnutrition. The weight began to fall from her frame like successive layers of skin, until there was almost nothing left of her. Within a short time, she was unable to stir from her place on the floor. I brought her water, and as she was too weak for words, I tried to tell her stories, though mine were never as good as hers.

On the last night of her life, our meal was a small piece of bread, torn into bite-sized scraps. There was one piece for each of us. She handed hers to me, clasping my fingers one last time, and smiled. Then her eyelids fluttered shut, and as I crouched at her side and ate, she quietly slipped away. I consider her martyrdom as heroic as Matangini's, and as great a gift to the soul of India.

In the aftermath of the great tribulations, my immediate task was to lift myself from the mud and take the first, determined steps toward an education of mind, body, and spirit worthy of those who had risked or given their lives that I might be free. And so, I trudged off barefoot through the knee-deep muck each day, happy to find an open classroom within a four-mile walk from my home, repeating the mantra from Matangini, "Never give up."

6

What Dreams Are Made Of

"AND THERE WAS LIGHT."

Both the Vedas and the Bible, products respectively of the Indo-European and Semitic cultures, assert that the light of creation arose from the mind of God. If we make the paradigm shift to conceiving God as an undivided, all-pervading entity, rather than a distant, finite being, then what would the mind of God look like? Perhaps it would be something like the cosmic consciousness of which the *rishis* spoke.

In the cosmology of the Vedas, the first thing Brahman uttered into the void was a sound: om. The Torah and, later, the Gospel of St. John, also suggest that God's breath carried a word (Logos), and they tie creation to the naming of things. Either way, we find the striking notion that material reality arises from conscious intent: the idea of a thing comes before the thing itself. In the fourth century BCE, Plato reached the same conclusion by way of reason rather than revelation, and his thinking later influenced Christianity and perhaps Eastern belief systems as well.

More than two millennia after Plato, these same strains
of thought found their way, albeit more humbly, into the
mind of a thin, barefoot adolescent slogging his way to
and from school with plenty of stops for daydreaming. I
sought, admittedly, to apply them toward a more personal
sort of creation. I wanted to be free of the constant pangs
of hunger in my belly and the fear that my home and my
few belongings might not be there when I returned from
school. The education by which I was eventually able to
turn knowledge into gold began with an idea: to study my
way out of poverty.

When I enrolled in high school, I took to math and science courses like the proverbial duck to water. The elegant
symmetry of math and the pristine logic of science drew
me with an almost magnetic force, and I had — even
then — a strong intuition that they were to be the basis
of my dreamed-of fortune.

I studied long after the conch shell had blown and the
oil lamp was lit for the night, and I quickly moved ahead
of other students. Before the math teacher had finished
writing a problem on the blackboard, I had solved it, and
soon enough, people were saying, "The Bhaumik boy
is a genius." If I had indeed earned this commendation,
then surely the 90 percent of perspiration factor was as
responsible for it as the 10 percent of inspiration.

The sign that I had become my math instructor's favorite pupil came in the form of an invitation to lunch at the
home where he resided with a family of high-caste Brah-
mins. This was the equivalent of a boy from South Central
Los Angeles being asked to dine in Beverly Hills.

I was, of course, thrilled, but my sense of newfound status turned to shame when I arrived and saw that my place had been set about six feet away from the others. Not even my teacher was willing to sit with me in violation of the time-honored code; not even my "genius" compensated for my caste. Nonetheless, I accepted my station and ate my meal with gratitude. I realized that he had taken a social risk simply by inviting me, even if only to put me on display for his aristocratic friends as a monkey who could work math problems. When lunch was finished, I quietly rose and took my plate to the pond to wash it, while servants washed the other plates. I somehow knew that one day my time would come.

Westerners look at the Hindu caste system and rightfully pronounce it inhumane or even laughably primitive, but they might look in their own backyards, as well. "Why did they ever put up with it?" people ask, but they could just as reasonably ask why proud African tribesmen put up with slavery. We might as well inquire as to why the moon doesn't come crashing into the Earth, for the answer may be surprisingly scientific.

Isaac Newton taught us that once things are set in motion they tend to stay in motion unless confronted by an opposing force. Once things have rigidified they remain rigid until pushed — or broken. In a social context as in a revolution, only great, primal forces such as hunger can shake people from such inertia, and then only if the forces are yoked to a powerful idea. Gandhi's movement represented such a marriage of instinct and ideal, but it takes time to shift the weight of the ages.

Even a revolutionary like my father, who rejected the caste system on ideological grounds, was forced to acknowledge it as a part of day-to-day life. As a teacher and a man who had received Gandhi's tutelage, however, he was in the grip of a greater force. On one occasion, our entire family was excluded from a village function and ceremony simply because my father had drunk water that an untouchable had fetched for him. Our neighbors agreed that the only remedy was a public apology and a dip in the Ganges River to absolve us of the taint of corruption.

My father refused to see his family do penance for a blameless act, and so we remained marginalized until about the time my grandmother died. The famine was then at its peak, and he used his persuasive powers to procure enough food from the local relief agency for the village to hold a veritable feast. Needless to say, our neighbors felt obliged to lift the sanctions before coming to the table. "Enough punishment," an elder proclaimed. "You are invited back into society." The force of hunger overcame the inertia of custom.

Neither my teacher's advocacy nor this small social victory erased the stigma of my birth, however. My steady progress at school earned me dubious compliments such as, "I'd let you marry my sister if only you were a Brahmin." The caste system was so deeply rooted that it seemed as if the ground of India herself would have to shift before we were freed from its legacy of social bondage. But great dreams have the power to break down prison doors. To live in the time of Mohandas Gandhi was to dream such dreams. To see what he accomplished was to believe all things are possible.

The newspapers reported that Gandhi was again on the brink of death. His tiny, emaciated frame — barely five feet five inches in height — appeared even smaller in the expanse of the prison yard, against the brick wall where he had come to rest like a blown leaf, trembling between flesh and spirit. His voice, for those close enough to hear it, was a whisper as rarefied as the air in Tibet. He was starving himself for the sake of those who had no voice at all: the untouchables.

This was the singular thing about Gandhi: he made his revolution not only against India's colonial masters, but against the native prejudices that kept her people even more insidiously enslaved. In the midst of an uprising against a common foe, he had stopped to turn his fearless gaze, and his *Satyagraha,* upon us, his people. "It has always been a mystery to me," he said, "that men can feel themselves honored by the humiliation of their fellow [human] beings." Gandhi believed that intolerance sprouted like a weed from a lack of self-esteem, that we were so jealous of our status yet privately fearful of our own worthlessness that we projected that fear onto the "other," in this case the lowest caste in Indian society.

Notwithstanding his humble loincloth and his otherworldly serenity, Gandhi was a brilliant political strategist. He had been a successful lawyer and had waged a bruising fight against apartheid in South Africa. He knew that an India at war with itself could never oust the Raj, and he saw the irony implicit in the fact that a nation of about four-hundred million allowed itself to be dominated by a handful of colonial occupiers. The movement had to be broadened to embrace all levels of Indian society, and the method by which he accomplished this was twofold: he bartered with his own life, and he effected a nationwide shift in perception of social realities.

By applying a new label to an old category — calling the untouchables *Harijan,* God's people — and including himself among them, Gandhi brought fifty to sixty million souls from the ragged margins of society into the body of the revolution. His near-fatal hunger strike, witnessed by the world, forged an eerily powerful mass relationship with the nation and broke the caste system's stranglehold. For the first time in thousands of years, orthodox temples were opened to the untouchables. Gandhi had become, through faith in action, the soul of India.

I have dwelt on this event not only because it was a turning point in the freedom movement nor because Gandhi's identification with the lowliest of my neighbors made it possible for me to imagine a life unshackled from the mark and poverty of my birth but because Gandhi's shifting of perceptions is a useful analogy when discussing the status of God in the age of science. For it is possible, to paraphrase Mark Twain, "the rumors of his death have been greatly exaggerated."

Most human beings, after all, still perceive God as a *personage* of one sort or another, even though we have traveled far beyond both Mt. Olympus and Mount Sinai, and it is that personification — a vestige of paganism — that turns many people away from spirituality. Perhaps we simply need to do as Gandhi did with the untouchables. Perhaps we need to call God by a new name.

The first decade of my life was shaped by India's burgeoning struggle for independence, by the fear and longing engendered by my father's absences, and by the ever-present threat of violence, as well as by the hope implanted in my breast by people like Matangini Hazra. As I crossed into my second decade, the pot of revolution had boiled over, and I had come to know heartbreak personally. Through it all, the ember of spiritual desire was never cold. It was to be fanned into flame in the presence of a man who had already forever altered my world, a man Einstein eulogized this way: "Generations to come, it may be, will scarce believe that such a one as this ever in flesh and blood walked upon this earth."

7

In the Court of the Naked King

ON AUGUST 8, 1942, GANDHI, who had shed his British-made suit and stripped down to the loincloth that became the symbol of his humility, deployed the "Quit India" slogan against the Raj. The words were polite, but the determination behind them was unmistakable and the timing propitious, for Britain was fully engaged in fighting Nazi Germany. Winston Churchill, who called Gandhi a "half-naked fakir," might assert that he "had not become the King's first minister in order to preside over the liquidation of the British Empire," but in many ways India was lost to England long before Gandhi demanded that the British "quit" her. I believe that the Raj was ultimately defeated by a power far greater than military might: Gandhi's intercession — through prayer, patience and fasting — with a stronger source behind all. We might say "The Source was with him."

A potent symbol of the revolution's victory from within was the sudden appearance in every home of the *charkha,* a portable spinning wheel that Gandhi designed himself. Under British dominion, India had been forced to ship her raw textiles off to Manchester, England, where cloth was manufactured and then sold back to India at inflated prices. Gandhi saw that to deny a people self-sufficiency was to keep them enslaved, and he exhorted all Indians to make their own *khadi,* an inexpensive cotton fabric. When he appeared on the cover of *Life* magazine, seated at a spinning wheel in his loincloth, it seemed that the world paused for a moment in its rotation.

Matangini and my father taught me to spin the *charkha,* giving me my first taste of the thrill of rightful insurrection as well as an inkling of the relativity of "social sin." Under the Raj, it was a punishable crime to spin, since in effect we were boycotting British textiles. But it was more than a practical lesson or an act of political defiance, for in the wheel's steady rotation with its impression of solid matter dissolving into a humming smear of energy and the emergence of yarn from raw fiber, I found a way to visualize the abstract notion that all is Brahman, that all substance derives from a single essence.

Beyond this, the act of spinning itself was conducive to meditation, a fact that Gandhiji surely had in mind when he said, "The music of the spinning wheel will be as balm to your soul."

This is not the book with which to examine Gandhi's argument in favor of experiential education, which held, in part, that the illumination of both intellect and spirit could begin with the study of the spinning wheel. But in view of the scientific territory ahead, it might be well to note that India is the home of the *charkha* (spinning wheel) and possibly of the chakra (wheel) as well, and it is also the land where the concept of zero as a number was first introduced and understood. India is a land of circles.

During Gandhi's last great push to rid India of its colonial overlords, he brought his teeming entourage to a place near Tamluk and made camp. It was my great fortune to live with him, to drink the wisdom that came from his lips, and to serve him for a short while. I have had a long life, rich in experience, but the events I am about to describe are close to the core of what I later became.

I was fourteen, and, because of the service that my father and Matangini had done for the movement, I was privileged to be able to volunteer my own labor in the camp. I was further privileged to sit near the small wooden platform from which Gandhiji spoke quietly to the gathering throngs each afternoon.

A roiling sea of people, hundreds upon hundreds of thousands, quietly waited for hours to get a distant glimpse of Gandhiji's diminutive form on the dais. As he spoke barely above the level of polite conversation, it was necessary to draw near in order to hear him, even when he used a microphone. This only made his words all the richer, because it was as if he were speaking to you. He couched his statements in the present tense, never reminiscing about his triumphs or bemoaning his many tragedies, never anticipating a future that had not yet occurred.

His eyes were gentle, his elfin face tirelessly animated by the beauty of his thoughts. He had a high forehead and oversized ears, and his upper lip was a narrow pen stroke nearly crossed by the tip of his nose. When he smiled, as he often did, he revealed toothless gums, for he wore his dentures only when the practical consideration of eating demanded it (once finished with his meal, he washed the dentures in full view of all of us, and I recall being struck by how steady his hands were). Four-fifths naked in his loincloth, he was the least self-conscious man I have ever encountered, and his utter lack of bodily vanity made it that much easier to see the glow of his spirit.

Gandhi, who had once worn pinstriped trousers with Savile Row suspenders, had become timeless India. To hear him speak of the Gita, and of how only the humble in spirit could be replenished by its grace, was to feel the way a teenaged boy in first-century Palestine might have felt as witness to the Sermon on the Mount.

After sunset, when the people had retired to their simple tents or to huts in far-flung villages, the camp became a field of light, torches twinkling through drifting mist and smoke in imitation of the stars just emerging from behind the veil of dusk. The peace that I felt at those times truly passes understanding, and the sense of protection was one I had rarely experienced in my father's house, for I was protected not only by the presence of an extraordinary man, but by an idea made manifest.

Dinner was a special time, because it was then that we could gather near and ask questions as he ate his simple meal, often no more than raisins and nuts and seldom consisting of ingredients beyond dates, lemons, oranges, peanuts, olive oil, and his staple, goat's milk. "There is no reason," he told us, "why you cannot reach the age of 125." The elements of longevity were a practiced detachment of mind, unselfish service to others, mud packs, plenty of sleep, occasional internal irrigation, and above all no alcohol, no stimulants, and no medicines. The regimens of many exclusive health spas owe much to Gandhi! Exercise was part and parcel of such a program (Gandhi thought nothing of walking fifty miles a day), and in Gandhi's case, celibacy was also.

By the time of our meeting, Gandhi had long been observing the discipline of *Bramacharya,* a strict abstention from meat, alcohol, and sex. His sublimation of sexual desire was believed to have given him great spiritual potency, but he had not always been so chaste. He had four sons, the second of whom, Manilal, my namesake, was part of his entourage in Tamluk. Kasturba (Kastur Ba), who had become Gandhi's wife when he was only thirteen, stood by him, a pillar of fortitude and forbearance in her own right. Although Gandhi now lived his conviction that "Paternalism is the root of all inequality," he and his beloved Ba had had their battles as man and wife before finding peace as equals united in soul. Their marriage was to last sixty-two years.

"What we think, we become," Gandhiji told us, and this is how he approached all quantum shifts in both material existence and consciousness. The leader, the great soul, who sat with us on the floor, his bare skin smooth and glowing with healthy color, was an effect of his own thought, a self-evolved individual. Could I, I wondered, ever think myself into a fuller life? At fourteen, it seemed a dream, but it is no secret where such dreams are made. We will speak later of how the agency of human consciousness can bring about a particular quantum reality, but while we are with Gandhi, it may be wise to hear his counsel, for Gandhi also spoke to us of God.

I was too young to have articulated the question "What is God?" to Gandhi, but I am certain that it was asked, and that he answered. When he spoke, he allowed us to enter his thinking process, never editing his thoughts, always keenly aware of the echoes that his words produced in our hearts. "There is an orderliness in the Universe, there is an unalterable law governing everything and every being that exists or lives. It is not a blind law, for no blind law can govern the conduct of human beings. The law that governs all life is God. Everything around us appears to change, but underlying that is a living power that is changeless; that holds together, creates, dissolves, and re-creates. That informing power or spirit is also God. God is life, truth, and love."

"But God (Brahman)," I might have protested, "is a name, like that of a person or an object. How can God be a law? How can God be love?"

The reply we received to such queries was a gentle smile, informing us that the answers would be evident when we were ready for them. And then, with his characteristic modesty, he said: "I have no special revelation of God's will. He reveals himself daily to each of us, but we shut our ears to the still, small voice."

To the question of how God can be a law, or love, or — as the Buddhists say — a no-thing, yet still be a presence we feel within our hearts almost as we feel the nearness of a loved one, I may be able to venture an answer now: God can be all these things if his nature is akin to that of

a *potentiality* rather than a definable state. Such a potentiality existed at the beginning of time and exists today at
the foundation of space.

After dinner, Gandhiji led the clean-up. The make-up of
our spiritual army ran the social gamut from untouchable
to Brahmin, but Gandhi insisted that all castes participate equally in even the most menial tasks. As you might
imagine in a social order as entrenched as India's, not
everyone acceded to this new paradigm with equal grace,
and more than one Brahmin had to be pulled by the ear to
the washtub, a spectacle that gave me and my group of
ragamuffins immeasurable delight.

No task aroused as much controversy or so graphically exemplified Gandhiji's new social order as did that
of cleaning his toilet. The younger volunteers like myself
saw it as a privi-lege (excuse the pun) and felt uniquely
honored when we were assigned the duty. Sometimes we
even competed with one another for this honor. Among the
older and more elevated of our company, emotions were
decidedly more mixed, but Gandhi was firm in his Zen-like
conviction that even the lowliest of tasks, if performed with
right attention and spirit, was sacred and further broke
down the barriers that separated us from one another.

He may have come by this conviction through an earlier
stand-off in his own marriage, for a well-known anecdote
tells of how Gandhi once nearly put his wife out of the
house for refusing to clean a public toilet. By the time
of the movement's ascendancy, even Kasturba had come
around.

As we followed him like ducklings around camp while he spun, sang, or walked, Gandhiji taught us much about the world, but he was careful to insist that literacy and knowledge for their own sake did not make for an education. "The sole purpose of education," he said, "is to bring out the best in us." By best, I believe he meant *that for which we were born.* Gandhi's notions of reform and renewal, whether at the personal or societal level, were based in his doctrine of *Sarvodaya,* which taught that real change must occur comprehensively, or, as we would now say, holistically, beginning in the heart and extending to the rim of the world.

I remembered his words, "Victory from within," and applied it to myself.

8

Out of the Black Hole

AS I WATCHED Gandhi and his entourage depart Tamluk, leaving me behind, I felt melancholy (and the longing to follow) that any child feels when the circus leaves town. After the exhilarating days in Gandhiji's camp, I felt stifled by both the social atmosphere and the limitations of the curriculum at my school. I asked my father to enroll me in a better school in Tamluk, but the cost was prohibitive. Fortune intervened when the headmaster of a distant school happened to read and admire my essay "The Formidable Twins: Famine and Epidemic."

The headmaster offered me board, and a friend of my father's offered me a bed, and these men, like Sarada and Matangini before them, provided lifelines of sustenance and moral support without which my story — not to say my survival — is unimaginable. Only those born within the fortress of privilege can maintain the illusion of self-sufficiency, and only then if they fail to look over the parapets into the streets below.

Those, like the young prince Siddhartha, who glimpse the struggle for existence beyond the palace walls can turn away only if their hearts are made of stone. Siddhartha became the Buddha, and though few of us are called to be saints, let alone Buddhas, I have come to believe that the happiest among us are those who employ their own good fortune to bring others closer to the light.

In 1947, the year I graduated from high school, British Raj at long last relinquished its grip on Mother India. Within six months, Gandhi was dead. He was fatally shot by one of his own, a fanatical Hindu nationalist who believed that Gandhi had betrayed his cause by allowing the partition of India that created the Muslim state of Pakistan.

Gandhiji was seventy-eight years old when he left us. His work was complete, and, as if in a quantum leap, European colonialism in Asia was, for all intents and purposes, finished. "What I did was a very ordinary thing," he said. "I declared that the British could not order me around in my own country." What he had done was anything but ordinary. He had exhausted an empire with the sheer force of his goodness. How, I still ask myself, does one accomplish that without the power of the heavens on his side?

As for me, I did not have the heavens, but, armed with an excellent score from my high school exam, I obtained a scholarship to study at the Scottish Church College in Calcutta. My years as a barefoot village boy were over, and I set off with a wary hope in my heart for a city as foreign to me as if it had been Paris, London, or New York. This fragile optimism was not based on any change in my material circumstances: I still had no money in my pocket and possessed only a single pair of shoes, a pair of pants, and a shirt. My fortune was in my mind; the education I had received had made me feel like an heir to some distant kingdom. And like all would-be kings, I began to dream of castles.

Christian missionaries ran the college, and it offered my first real encounter with the great Western faith. Gandhi had kept a picture of Jesus on a wall of his hut, and beneath it he had written, "He is our peace," but Gandhi had also insisted that "in the world beyond, there are neither Christians, Hindus, nor Muslims." It therefore came as a great surprise to me to discover that the Christian brothers who oversaw my schooling were every bit as certain as the most blindly devout Hindu or Muslim that theirs was the surest path to God.

Dr. John Kellas, the principal, was sensitive to my tradition, even presenting me once with a copy of the *Patrabali* (letters) of the great Indian teacher Vivekananda (also a graduate of the college), in which the swami asserted that "we are part of God." But when I pressed my instructors to reconcile this with the Christian doctrine of Original Sin, I got nowhere. Their tendency was to regard the faith of my ancestors as pagan, something ultimately to be washed away in the new tide.

Part of me bridled at this presumption, but another part of me was drawn to the Christian message: "We are all created in the image of God." This conflict provoked my first serious spiritual crisis. If I chose one faith, must I reject the other? And what would my choice say about who I was? Was there no way I could leave behind the backwardness of my village without also losing myself?

Though I owe much to the Scottish brothers, I now know that they failed as spiritual unifiers. More perceptive teachers might have cited the parallels between Vedic spirituality and much of what Jesus taught. It was especially hard for me to accept that an innocent child is born in sin without having done anything to deserve such a blemish. Curiously, during the same time, a wiser soul, soon to be known to the world as Mother Teresa of Calcutta, was enacting her profound belief, "Each child is created in the special image of God for great things — to love and to be loved." Even as a Christian missionary, she discerned God's love in each person — whether a Hindu, a Muslim or a Christian. An unquestionable spiritual unifier, she made everyone who came to know her feel a personal kinship regardless of faith or religious background. But such pan-religious thinking was not in evidence at the college.

What I needed to break through my cloud cover of confusion was a mediating perspective — a bird's eye view — from which I could see that the many paths of deep and genuine belief converged upon a single point. Paradoxically, I found this perspective in the outer reaches of what most people perceived of as the antithesis of religion: science.

Although Albert Einstein presented his special theory of relativity in 1905 (and the general theory in 1915), the world of 1949–1950 had not yet digested its momentous implications, other than to receive a terrible proof in the form of the atomic bomb. Upon the first successful test of the atomic bomb at Alamogordo, New Mexico, team leader J. Robert Oppenheimer is said to have uttered a line from the Bhagavad Gita: "I am become Death, the destroyer of the world." Scientists, and especially teachers of science, were still struggling to fathom Einstein's revelation, but one thing was understood: the sharp line between the material and the immaterial had been blurred — if not erased — by the famous equation $E = mc^2$.

Until Einstein came along, it was assumed that mass and energy were entirely separate things. What we had not perceived was that everything is made of energy. Up to the time I encountered $E = mc^2$, I could not reconcile in my mind how a "physical" thing like a human body could be home to an abstract entity such as consciousness.

The separation of mind and matter, which had prevailed in the West since the time of Descartes, seemed arbitrary, and it conflicted with my tradition; by what scientific principle could they be joined? Once I had grasped Einstein's assertion of the equivalence of mass and energy — by which a "concrete" thing is presumed to consist of an abstract substance — it suddenly made sense to me that body and mind could comprise a whole that was simultaneously material and spiritual.

If this were true, then we really might be — as the old *rishis* had said — souls with bodies rather than bodies with souls. You might ask, "What's the difference?" After all, the words are simply flip-flopped, aren't they? But the distinction is critical. If the spiritual aspect is primary and the material secondary, then it is a very different kind of universe indeed, and religious differences are mostly beside the point.

With his simple equation, Einstein lit the trailhead of spirituality through science, a path I have been following ever since. "Religion without science," he said, "is blind" and "science without religion is lame."

As complex organisms grow from a single cell, entire philosophies can develop from a single idea. In the light of my altered worldview, the most dramatic events of my life made a new kind of sense. Gandhi had not been merely a man of flesh and blood suffering for his nation, but a spirit that hungered for a lasting peace. Matangini had died in a hail of bullets, but her spirit had found its everlasting freedom. And my grandmother, who had given her last morsel of bread that I might live, had bestowed the supreme gift of spiritual love. Peace, freedom and love: I did not know it then, but these are everything the heart requires.

After graduating from the Church College, I pursued a master's degree at the University of Calcutta, where my beloved mentor was Satyendra Nath Bose, already world famous for his role in formulating the Bose-Einstein statistics. Physicist and Nobel laureate Paul Dirac named a class of elementary particles "boson" after him.

On one unforgettable occasion, Dirac came to our university to lecture on what became known as quantum field theory. Although the math went straight over my head, the notion that discrete subatomic particles — the matter of which we are made — arose from a totally abstract continuum struck me as even more sublime than Einstein's equation of mass and energy, and I was as enchanted as a young sailor experiencing the allure of hearing his first siren song. I wanted to follow that song, but my father had other plans for me.

My father thought I had achieved all that people of our station should dare to hope for, and he asked me to return to the village and take up his mission as a schoolteacher. For a time, I acceded to his wish, but I had already seen farther into life's possibilities than it had ever been his fortune to see, and I was deeply restless. Moreover, I found it hard to take my mind where it wanted to go on an empty stomach. I had dreamt of my mansion on a hilltop, and I believed — naively, it turned out — that if only I could get there, a vast, blue sky of happiness would open before me. Wealth, like food, seems indispensable only when you don't have it, but you can't tell that to a young man who has seen his castle shimmering in the distance.

In 1954, I received some good news and a rare bit of poetic justice. I was offered a scholarship, courtesy of the government of independent India, to conduct research for my Ph.D. in physics at the Indian Institute of Technology (IIT). The laboratory I would use was directly adjacent to the grounds of the infamous internment camp in which my father had been held during the years of struggle for independence.

A stipend of 150 rupees was provided for my living expenses, more money than I had ever seen. As I was still a long way from acquiring expensive tastes, I sent some of it back to my family. It gave me great satisfaction to look out the laboratory windows and ponder that a country, whose colonial overlords had imprisoned my father, was now free and helping to make his load a little lighter.

All great universities open up vistas of thought and self-discovery to those willing to explore. To be encouraged to pursue one's deepest questions wherever they lead is perhaps the greatest gift any young man or woman can receive. I had never felt so free to follow my heart.

My scientific worldview, stirred into being by that first, unblinded sight of the night sky, gestated by revolution, loss, and spiritual heroism, and midwived by Einstein, Bose, and Dirac, was now to mature. Science gives us the means to see in dimensions beyond the familiar, among them the realm of invisible reality. I began to perceive that this landscape was every bit as intriguing as the world of what we can touch and feel.

My energies as a doctoral candidate at IIT were not entirely consumed by a love of science. India, perhaps more than any other place, gives equal play to the intensely cerebral, the sublimely spiritual, and the dizzyingly sensual. I had been carrying a torch in my heart, as had so many aspiring troubadours before me, for a girl "above my station," a lovely, bewitching girl I'd grown up with and had long wished secretly to make my own. Now, surely — I thought — she will see past the mud floor of my birth and the mark of my caste to who I truly am: a future hero of scientific discovery. In that precipitous rush that the heart makes toward its desire, I asked her to be my wife. Her reply is etched in my memory to this day.

"How could you even think of such a thing," she said, unamused. "Everyone knows you have no money, no prestige or social connections. What do you suppose my family would say?" She shook her pretty head as if to say, "You just don't get it," and walked away.

An older, wiser man might have weighed this callous response in his heart and concluded that such a girl was not likely to become my own version of Gandhiji's beloved Ba. But I had no wisdom in such matters, and my self-esteem suffered a devastating blow. For months, I did not speak to another girl. I could not attribute the slight to her ignorance, only to my inferiority, and with the zeal of a soldier wielding a ramrod against the palace gates, I strapped my intellect to the pursuit of fame and fortune.

An ironic postscript to this story is that years later, after I had achieved a measure of success in California, a delegate from the same girl's family approached me with an offer of her hand in marriage — now that I was "suitable." In the most charmingly diplomatic manner I could summon, I demurred. By that time, I was genuinely beyond taking any satisfaction from the turnabout, but the young man in me was healed of an old wound.

I was no monk, but science had by then become, and would largely remain, my chosen consort, and marriage was far from my sights. Still, I took the event as evidence that few of the wishes we make in the past are without some corresponding symmetry in the present or future. The girl went on to marry someone else, and we remain friends.

Throughout my period of growth and discovery at IIT, I was exposed to a cosmopolitan array of experts and scholars from the West, principally from Cold War adversaries America and the Soviet Union, as well as from several European countries. The students also came from all corners of India. My provincial outlook started to fade in this ecumenical atmosphere.

In 1958 I received my Ph.D., the first the school awarded. That same year, I was publishing in the *American Journal of Chemical Physics.* Also published in the same journal was an article by William McMillan, UCLA's renowned professor of chemical physics. I was impressed with what he wrote.

My burning ambition was now to go to the United States, specifically California, to study with him. Based on Dr. Bose's recommendation, Professor McMillan offered me a Sloan Foundation Fellowship to underwrite my living expenses at UCLA. However, as so often happened in my struggle to extricate myself from the black hole of poverty and a destiny shackled to social status, there was a Catch-22.

The expenses were to be paid only after my arrival at UCLA, but the airfare was completely beyond my reach! It seemed I was to experience the bitterest of ironies, one known all too well to the hundreds of millions trapped in the cycles of despair. Somewhere on that distant, golden shore a mansion stood on a hill with my name engraved above the brass door knocker, but for lack of the means to buy a ticket, I would never set foot in it.

I thought of some well-to-do acquaintances in Calcutta, and I approached them with hat in hand. "This is a fool's errand," they told me. In their estimation, no village boy could hope to grow so far beyond his roots. They sent me away empty-handed and I returned to the village sick at heart.

Fittingly enough, it was my roots — the village itself — that lifted me toward the sun, for in a scene straight out of the classic film *It's a Wonderful Life* my neighbors came one-by-one to my father's hut, offering whatever they had, so one of their own might finally taste a better life. It was a gift I will seek to reciprocate for all of my days.

If you allow me a scientific analogy, the world of 1959 had not yet been properly introduced to black holes, those collapsed stars whose gravitational fields are so powerful that nothing, not even light, can escape them. It took the genius of Stephen Hawking to show that certain particles (known as Hawking radiation) can actually find their way out of these cosmic sinkholes.

As a boy, I'd known nothing of such spacetime anomalies, but nonetheless I had lived daily with the fear one imagines an interstellar traveler might feel as his ship drops over the event horizon of a black hole on its way to a crushing oblivion. In those days, I couldn't conceive of any way to exit the black hole of poverty. I know now that, for a lucky few, escape is possible, as in Hawking radiation. I was on my way to the heart of my dreams.

9

Lasers in Bloom

I ARRIVED in Los Angeles with three dollars in my pocket.

As I crossed the runway's tarmac, clutching a frayed overnight bag to my breast like a shield, I became aware of conflicting sensations. The powdery caress of Pacific air on my face on that soft spring day promised miracles. But the anxious rumbling of my stomach signaled both an abstract apprehension and a very real hunger.

I was hardly the first immigrant to face the New World without knowing where he would take his first meal or spend his first night, but every new arrival must feel a little like the first. And each of our stories, though knitted by common humanity, is unique in the details of its telling.

The first proof of just how far I'd traveled from Tamluk came when I left the gate and found Professor McMillan himself there to receive me. Such treatment would never have been accorded to a young man of my station in India. The professor had not seen even a photograph of me, but he had no trouble picking the lanky young Indian with the worn bag and wide eyes out of the crowd. His welcome put me right at ease, but it was his Cadillac convertible that told me I'd found the land of milk and honey.

I had never seen such a car! It was three times the size of anything on the narrow streets of Indian cities, let alone in my village, where oxcarts still often had the right of way. Beyond that, Professor McMillan initiated me into the American cult of speed from the moment he ramped onto the freeway. Feeling the thrust of a V-8 at eighty miles per hour would have made my hair stand on end even if the wind had not. He booked me into a nice hotel near UCLA, where I finally caught my breath and marveled that I, who'd only recently been deemed unsuitable for marriage, had been received like visiting royalty!

In the bright morning, I was taken out to find an apartment, and I gazed for the first time on the streets that I would one day cruise in my own convertible. I was dazzled by the lushly landscaped and cultivated West Side of Los Angeles. We navigated Sunset Boulevard through Beverly Hills and Bel Air, places that meant nothing to me then but which I would soon learn were fitting places for a man to build his palace. There were secret, shaded enclaves that whispered of romance and riches, and sun-gilded hilltops suitable for Kubla Khan himself! With my face pressed to the car window, I picked out one after another. That one! No, that one is higher! Ah, but surely this one must have an ocean view! In my jet-lagged ecstasy, I had momentarily forgotten that my wallet was empty.

By the time we arrived at the Chemistry Building, sobriety had returned with a gnawing hunger and a growing panic about how I was to sustain myself. Anxiously, I asked Professor McMillan whether I might possibly have an advance against my scholarship monies, and to my astonished relief, he agreed without hesitation. Would wonders never cease? No sooner had my stomach been filled than my imagination returned to those hilltops.

If the place of one's birth is always home in our cells' memory, then it can also be said that the spirit may find its home in a far country. I flourished in America from the beginning because I sensed quickly that there even the most lofty ambition was encouraged if backed up by a will to work hard, whereas in India ambition was often seen as overreaching pride.

For those born in the United States, the truth of the American dream may be so obvious as to be missed, but for an immigrant from a nation still draped in centuries of regressive custom, it is nothing less than revelation. Its essence is stunningly simple: If you are good at your work, all doors open. It doesn't matter whether you were born in a hut or in a château. What matters is what you produce. Perhaps nowhere is this truer than in California. In California even the sunlight seemed to be raw material for building dreams.

My life, like that of most people, has been shaped by a series of living examples, and Professor McMillan quickly became one of them. I had never seen anyone push himself so relentlessly. In hindsight, I suppose he was what people call a workaholic; how else to explain that often the best time to corner him for a conference was at 2:00 a.m. in the campus library!

I studied his habits as diligently as I studied his lessons, determined not only to learn everything he knew about advanced physics but to emulate his drive toward discovery and success. As at IIT, my research was in electronic energy transfer, but the new insights that Professor McMillan encouraged required a diligence and dedication to math that all but blotted thoughts of spiritual matters from my mind for a while.

Looking back, it may be that having as my first American role model a man as fiercely industrious as Professor McMillan took me farther from my roots than might have been the case under the tutelage of a pure theorist, but a pure theorist would not have pushed me to the escape velocity I sought to achieve. I wanted to be as far from the pull of that black hole as possible.

There had been a period before my departure when I did seriously question whether my thirst for education and accomplishment was a betrayal of my spiritual heritage, to be slaked at the cost of enlightenment. Strange as it may seem to those accustomed to a mercantile culture that pays only lip service to transcendence, the highest goal for a Hindu remains that of achieving oneness with God through renunciation of the world. The most revered figures are those ascetics who seek a life free of illusion. Although I'd chosen a path of science rather than self-abnegation, the pull of the spirit toward its maker — the eternal song of India — was never entirely absent from my heart.

For now, however, breaking free of the awful gravity of my past left me feeling virtually weightless. In America's sunny, egalitarian climate, I began to shed my inferiority complex. Piece by piece, the shell of caste and social shame fell away, and I emerged, a gangly butterfly with wet, wrinkled wings. On my very first weekend in Los Angeles, I had a date to meet a pretty UCLA co-ed at the corner of Westwood and Wilshire Boulevard in Westwood Village, and though it wasn't the sort of hooking up that college students casually arrange these days, I was dizzy with joy. She was waiting for me, radiating friendliness in the inimitable way that American girls do, and she was happy — even eager — to see me!

I was nearly thirty, and I had never experienced the thrill of having a woman regard me as romantically desirable.

When our first date went well, we continued seeing each other. Just as Professor McMillan was my mentor in matters of study and enterprise, she became my tutor in matters of love. She helped me to overcome my painful shyness, and I was never again ashamed of having amorous appetites. Our friendship continued even after she transferred to UC Berkeley.

My early years in America coincided with the coming into office of the charismatic young president John F. Kennedy. It was a bracing, hopeful time, filled with talk of moon landings and of liberation for the millions struggling under the Soviet boot. But it was also a time of social unrest not unlike what I'd experienced in Bengal, for here in the streets of my soon-to-be-adopted country a great movement had arisen for the civil rights of black people, America's own untouchables, led by a man very much guided by Gandhi's example. I recognized in the Reverend Martin Luther King those same qualities of abiding conviction and patient tenacity that had characterized Gandhiji, and I knew that ultimately his movement would prevail.

Many Americans of that day bristled at the suggestion that their homegrown prejudice was cousin to the institutionalized discrimination in India. I was made starkly aware of this on the day of my arrival, when a kindly white immigration officer, escorting me through Customs, asked me casually how it was that Indians could tolerate an outrage like the caste system. I replied that there was no logical basis for it, just as there was no logical basis for mistreatment of black people in America. The rest of our business was conducted in stony silence, and I realized that I had touched a sore spot.

Not long after I had settled in Los Angeles, I offered to help a newly arrived friend from India find an apartment. My friend was quite dark skinned and, naively, I hadn't imagined that racial prejudice crossed ethnic lines. Upon entering the rental office of one modest complex, the landlady, a thin, bitter woman, took one look at us, scowled, and said, "Didn't you know this is a white house?" "No," I replied, not intending to be cheeky. "I thought that was in Washington, D.C." We were promptly shown the door.

Because of my own struggle to overcome social determinism — the notion that one's birth status could bar him from freedoms and opportunities others had — I have always felt a profound empathy for those whom society deems "marked." It is my conviction that we are all, as Gandhiji had said, "a part of God," and that any sins we bear result from our failure to realize this and act accordingly. Martin Luther King, to the day of his tragic death, seemed to me a man who also grasped this truth. Black people had suffered subjugation for centuries, and although King did not get to see his dream come true, his civil rights movement in America bore fruit within decades, as if by a quantum leap.

Much as I identified with the fight for racial equality, I had not escaped Tamluk in order to reprise its struggles. Amid the social tumult and intellectual stimulation of those first years, my driving ambition remained to free myself once and for all from poverty, and there is one event that I still recall with the clarity of a dream.

I had just obtained my driver's license and was at the wheel of my girlfriend's car, cruising Sunset Boulevard on a beautiful afternoon. I made a wrong turn and we suddenly found ourselves in a lushly wooded enclave, facing an enormous gate. On the pillar of the gate were letters that read "Bel Air." I turned to my companion and said, "This is where I will live one day." Although I had no crystal ball, developments occurring at places like Bell Labs, Hughes Research, and Columbia University would make my statement prophetic.

Within one year of my arrival in the United States the new field of laser technology opened up, and I dove in. LASER is an acronym for Light Amplification by Stimulated Emission of Radiation, a real mouthful. We will stick to laser! Laser development utilized information from the specialized field of electronic energy transfer, which had been the subject of my Ph.D. dissertation as well as my studies at UCLA. The added fact that a laser beam is an example of what is called *boson condensation,* named for my mentor Satyendra Nath Bose, cemented my feeling of a strong affinity for this bold new technology.

Early science fiction writers like H. G. Wells and pioneering inventors like Nikola Tesla had envisioned laser-like death rays that could instantly vaporize anything in their path. Einstein himself had derived the basic principle of the laser as early as in 1917. But the notion that photons of light could be stimulated to produce a powerful and highly directed beam capable of precision cutting through materials as hard as steel or as delicate as human tissue was not given serious attention. That was until Charles Townes and his students at Columbia University accomplished a similar feat with microwave radiation in the mid-1950s, dubbing it the MASER. The challenge then became to achieve the same results with the shorter wavelengths of visible light, and this was done in 1960, when Theodore Maiman demonstrated the first ruby laser at the Hughes Research Laboratory in Malibu.

It is all about coherence, a word that describes the state of things "holding together as one." Because this word will play a key part in the discussion of how to attain elevated consciousness through meditation, I will offer a (mercifully) brief description of how a laser works. Even for those not technically oriented, it's worth the effort of comprehension; just imagine what your mind could accomplish if it were as focused as a laser beam.

The basic idea is remarkably simple. An ordinary beam of light, which is emitted in units called photons, is incoherent. Even when it is focused, such as in a high-powered searchlight, much of the light is lost by diffusion. Not even the most powerful searchlight can hit the moon. But there is no use crying over spilled photons. Instead, we need to find a way to martial them into phase — to make them coherent.

In a laser, a material known as an active medium is placed into a cavity. The first lasers used solids such as rubies or gasses like helium-neon. The atoms of this material, the active medium, are then brought into a higher state of excitation by bursts of energy. In solid and liquid lasers, such excitation is provided by a flash gun, like that on a camera, in a process known as optical pumping.

Taking a gas laser as an example, picture a narrow glass tube with mirrors at each end, one of them partially transparent. When the atoms of gas inside the tube are excited by electrical discharge, they spontaneously emit photons of light, as in a common neon lamp. But some photons will find themselves between the mirrors, and they will be reflected back and forth at the speed of light, stimulating other atoms to give up photons, as well. It is a bootstrapping process, feeding on itself, which reaches ever higher levels of intensity and eventually takes on its own steam. The light begins to lase, and the army of photons, now in lockstep, exits the partially transparent mirror as a perfectly coherent beam of light capable of hitting a manhole cover on the surface of the moon.

In the final chapter of this book, we'll imagine that the diffuse cloud of thought in our own minds is analogous to the quasi-coherent (not holding together as one) light emitted before lasing begins, and ask what sort of transformation of consciousness might occur if we could similarly bootstrap our minds to greater coherence.

As marvelous as the laser's discovery was, its real-world applications were not immediately apparent, and for some time it was characterized as a solution in search of a problem. Few people then foresaw a world measured and probed, inscribed and read, cut and fused in technologies ranging from bar code scanners and DVD players to corneal sculpting, the last of which helped me to get through the gates of Bel Air.

My Ph.D. dissertation contained threads of information applicable to laser research and landed me an interview in Pasadena with Electro-Optical Systems, later acquired by Xerox. I was made a staff scientist there and my employer secured a permanent work visa for me, the first step toward planting my feet firmly in American soil. We began immediately developing a laser using the compound chelate, having received an unexpectedly huge grant from the U.S. Air Force. When a colleague and I presented our findings to the Third International Quantum Electronics conference in Paris, I was one long stride closer to the threshold of my mansion on a hill.

Although the chelate laser was soon overtaken as the gold standard in liquid laser research by the dye laser invented at IBM, Xerox felt strongly enough about my contribution to reward me with shares of its stock, a boon that provided my first taste of financial freedom. Nonetheless, I was crestfallen not to have won the big prize and to suddenly find myself merely one of many struggling for recognition.

The rivalries were fierce, the job stresses even fiercer, and I sometimes wondered whether I possessed the native resources to keep pace with my more competitively wired American colleagues. One day, when I was feeling particularly strung out, I found that — thanks to my heritage — I had in my ancestral kit bag a tool that Westerners were then only beginning to discover: meditation.

Without giving it much thought, I began to cool myself down by counting to one hundred in Bengali. I found a quiet place in my home, sat in a natural, comfortable position with my feet on the floor and my spine straight, and began to focus on the rhythm of each count. *Ac* (one) ... *dui* (two) ... *tin* (three) ... *char* (four) ... *punch* (five).

By the time I'd done a few rounds, I had crossed a threshold, though I was no more aware of the crossing than I am of the moment when sleep comes at night. Simply by attending to the act of silently counting I had dispelled superfluous thoughts and entered a meditative state, making a leap from one level of consciousness to another. After the end of meditation, I was so full of energy that I felt if I jumped I would probably land on the moon! When the time came for me to return to work, things had become manageable, for I was perceiving them from a different perspective, one that was not so close to my anxious core. Believe me, it took all of my restraint not to run through the office shouting, "Eureka!"

This ecstatic feeling, of course, wasn't my discovery, though it will always feel like a revelation to one experiencing it for the first time. Mystics throughout the ages have known this feeling, and my Indian forebears described it colorfully (and fittingly) as "bubbling from the inside." It is the great, divine calm that ensues when one has dimmed down the organs of sensory perception enough to feel re-connected to the ground of being, and it is remarkably accessible. The software is pre-installed.

From that modest start — relaxing and counting — I would eventually move on to deeper levels of meditation, and finally to the quantum leap I'll discuss in the final chapter of this book. Such breakthroughs, however, would not occur until I had learned from science certain amazing things about the nature of reality, such as the fact that the total energy of the universe adds up to zero! I will try to convey these wonders, grounded firmly in advanced physics, as painlessly as possible.

My original intent was to stay in America for only one year. The plan was for me to go back and serve my native land as a teacher and scientific researcher. By now, however, I found myself consumed by a fascination with laser technology and its development, and I was determined to make my mark. At the same time, I knew the knowledge I had acquired was highly sought in India. The conflict between my ambition and my sense of duty became so great that I began to suffer splitting headaches. In a fore-shadowing of the spiritual crisis to come years later, I felt myself being torn in two. In 1964, after five years in America, I took a leave of absence from Xerox and returned to my native land as a draftee in a pool of foreign-trained scientists.

Unexpectedly, it was during this time in India that I experienced one of the happiest times of my life. I found a contentment that was reminiscent of the week I had spent in the presence of Gandhi, but on a different level.

There was no pressure from work so I was free to follow my interest. Due to the lack of adequate experimental facilities in India, I spent most of my time doing routine theoretical work on lasers and giving seminars. With my savings from America, I was able to live comfortably, at least by Indian standards. This gave me the opportunity to practice meditation regularly and for long stretches of time. Although this may sound boring, once I had a taste of the nectar, I wanted more.

I had my deepest mystical experiences during this time. But these intensely blissful states faded as soon as it became necessary to interact with people who were on a completely different wavelength from me, caught up in their own daily struggles. No wonder the *rishis* retreated to Himalayan caves! Though the state of bliss was interrupted, my meditations paid dividends. I was able to feel and act afterward with an exquisite lucidity of mind, and this held more appeal for me than merely being blissed out. I wondered what it might be like to work, to live, and to love in such a relaxed but highly attentive state. What things might be seen that were normally missed?

It was with this clarity of mind that I affirmed science to be my true calling. To honor the sacrifices that my grandmother and the people of my village had made on my behalf, I knew that I must redeem the hope they'd placed in me. In India, I was far from the cutting edge of laser research. The fruit of this research was sure to be a gift to humankind. I wanted to be where I could best contribute, and that place was America. Thus it was a brief homecoming, for a fire had been lit inside me.

10

In Quantum Leaps

AS IN THE GLORY DAYS of Silicon Valley, developments in the laser field were occurring at warp speed, and those not fully committed were liable to be left on the sidelines. To be in the forefront of any endeavor is exhilarating, but I felt driven by more than competitive zeal. I suppose it was a kind of existential terror: I knew that the black hole would swallow me up if I failed.

As if to affirm that I'd sailed beyond the point of return, I declared the United States to be my adopted country, and in 1966 I bought my first home. It was a real house of timber and brick, one that no cyclone could destroy and in which I felt secure from peril. (I had not yet experienced my first Los Angeles earthquake!) It was also my first, modest foray into the lucrative world of California real estate, a fascination that later became a hobby and then a sort of grand obsession. Before too long, I had begun to trade my Xerox shares for something even more substantial: Golden State land.

For the next year, I continued to work for Xerox's Electro-Optical Systems, hoping to set the next benchmark in laser technology. That opportunity, however, did not come until later.

There is a tenet of modern scientific philosophy, which argues that great advances in knowledge do not occur solely through trial and error, but await the occurrence of intuition and the readiness of the human mind. In other words, to quote the tagline of the television show *The X-Files,* "The truth is out there." It is a matter of perceiving it. This may help to explain how and why epochal shifts such as the invention of the wheel, Greek philosophy, the Renaissance, and modern science came about. It may be that this is no less applicable to breakthroughs in human spirituality than to the kind of discoveries that my colleagues and I were about to make in the field of laser technology.

In 1968, I was invited to join the team at the Research and Technology Center of Northrop Corporation, a major aerospace contractor that offered extraordinary facilities for a working physicist. My raison d'être was now the carbon monoxide (CO) laser. Based on my research, my colleagues at Northrop demonstrated the most powerful continuous laser to date. In a further step forward, I was able to make the laser operate at room temperatures, something previously thought impossible.

Sitting in the hall on the day I presented my results to a UCLA seminar was Edward Teller, the man whose revelatory insights had earned him the title Father of the H-Bomb. Dr. Teller was so intrigued by my talk that when he felt nature's call and had to leave the room, he asked

that I suspend my talk until his return. My own validation as a scientist came when a Soviet scientist later wrote
in a prestigious Russian journal, "After Bhaumik's thor-
ough work on the CO laser, there isn't much left to do [on
that laser]." I now had international recognition, and with
recognition comes a license to move boldly. A group of
us embarked upon an exciting new project under the joint
auspices of Northrop, Maxwell Laboratories in San Diego,
and Los Alamos National Laboratories in New Mexico.

Among the dynamically talented international group of
co-workers that I assembled as manager of the laser technology lab at Northrop, the synergy was so great that we
felt there was no problem we couldn't solve. Our group
earned high esteem in the laser community, and we were
frequently invited to give lectures at laser symposia all
over the world. Eventually, my team and I hit the jackpot.

As the principal investigator and team leader, I had
the privilege of making our official announcement. On
March 14, 1973, at a meeting of the Optical Society of
America in Denver, I reported the conclusive demonstration of the world's first excimer laser, using xenon gas as
its active medium. This marvelous class of lasers was to
revolutionize surgery and help produce my lasting fortune.

One of the signature applications of the excimer laser
is in corneal sculpting, the corrective eye surgery best
known to most people under the trade name LASIK. The
cornea is the transparent outer layer of the eye. By care-
fully contouring a hair-thin layer of corneal tissue as one
would a contact lens, such conditions as nearsightedness
and farsightedness can be corrected. While most lasers

cut by burning, excimer lasers do a "cold cut," evaporating tissue cells without burning or risk to healthy tissue. The laser beam's "cut" goes no deeper than a superficial scratch on the skin. The entire procedure takes less than a minute, and you can go to work the next day.

Nowadays, the chances are good that you or someone you know may be reading this page without glasses or contacts thanks to corneal sculpting.

In recognition of my work in laser technology, I was elected by my peers to be a fellow of the American Physical Society as well as of the Institute of Electrical and Electronics Engineers. But the recognition that moved me most deeply came when my alma mater, IIT, awarded me an honorary DSc degree for lifetime academic achievement.

Northrop, in appreciation of my laser patents, handsomely compensated me with stock, which, given the company's performance, soon appreciated extravagantly. I was already dabbling in real estate and other investment strategies; now I became a serious player, expanding my portfolio to include stocks, bonds, futures, and options — in short, the whole enchilada. I wonder now if I took greater risks with money than more conventional investors because I'd already known the experience of having none.

In any case, this was the late 1970s. The California real estate boom was in full swing, and runaway inflation tied to rising oil prices made my gambling something better than a crap shoot. My properties became valuable beyond even my wildest expectations. It was more like a fable than it was like any real life I had imagined. At the age of fifty-five I took an early retirement from Northrop and set my sights on satisfying every desire that had ever seemed beyond my grasp.

My journey from mud to marble was complete, and like Fitzgerald's Jay Gatsby, I sought to wipe clean all traces of the poor immigrant boy I had been. Within just a few years, I owned six hilltop houses with million-dollar post-card views; Beverly Hills, Bel Air, Palos Verdes, Malibu — each one was a bulwark against the fate of my ancestors. I also drove a Rolls-Royce.

It was the realization of my most fervent hopes in every way but one. Neither my grandmother nor Matangini Hazra was alive to see that, indeed, rewards do come to those who never give up. They say that Elvis Presley bought his mother a pink Cadillac upon receiving his first recording contract. Had Sarada and Matangini been with me at this time, I would have found some way to put them in a Rolls-Royce Silver Cloud.

For some years to come, thoughts of cosmology and causation and the transcendent reality beyond all appearances were swept from my mind. I was on a merry-go-round.

II

The Merry-Go-Round Broke Down

LIFE IN THE FAST LANE doesn't get any faster — or more
hazardous — than in Los Angeles. New kings are crowned
every day, and old monarchies fall just as frequently. Here,
in the midst of the roaring eighties, I was freshly minted
royalty, and for a time I enjoyed every minute of it. Notwithstanding the spiritual imperative of my forebears, the
life of a monk was not for me, and even when the time
came to question the foundation of my existence, I did
not for a moment consider leaving the joys, tragedies,
and travesties of everyday life behind, only its ceaseless
hunger and conspicuous consumption.

For a time, however, I gave James Bond a run for his
money, and I lived out my own international version of the
Beach Boys' "California Girls."

In frosty, free-thinking Sweden, I loved a bright, uninhib-
ited soul named Anne. Later in glasnost-revitalized Russia,
I wooed charismatic Maria in faraway St. Petersburg. We
visited Calcutta together, and she fell in love with the City
of Joy. Later still on a junket to beautiful Milano, expa-
triate Astrid captured my heart, and after an enchanted

series of evenings at Lake Como, she, too, accompanied me to India.

I was not certain how Maria and Astrid would react to seeing that I had been born in a village of mud huts, but unlike Gatsby, I made no attempt to disguise my origins. For me, it was a matter of pride that I'd risen so far above them on my own steam. To my surprise (and my mother's delight), Astrid was enchanted with my birthplace, and my mother began to call her Nivedita, after the devoted disciple of Swami Vivekananda.

Because of my courtship with an actress named Roberta, I became an avid skier. We slalomed the powdery runs in Gstaad, Switzerland, and closer to home in Aspen, Snowmass and Snowbird. It never ceased to amaze me that I was able to schuss down the precipitous slopes with next to no training, having learned to walk in shoes only as an adolescent. Perhaps it was the result of all that slogging to and from school through ankle-deep mud!

A trip to the altar with one of the ladies may have seemed in the cards, but it was not to be. Every one of my relationships with women has enriched me, and each occupies a place in my heart, yet I knew even in the throes of devotion that I would never make good husband material. Truth be told, not many scientists do.

The lonely, monastic nature of the work and the single-minded pursuit of answers are liable to leave a wife feeling like a widow. Even while my body enjoyed the life of an international epicure, my mind had long been betrothed to science. A hermit's retreat in the Himalayas might not be for me, but I continued to crave intellectual altitudes where there is usually only enough oxygen for one.

Wealth and professional prominence foster social connections, and these connections can earn you a place on the best party lists in town. Being at ease on the A-list, however, required a sense of social entitlement that was quite foreign to me. (I didn't realize then how much of Los Angeles' aristocracy shared my humble origins.) So, instead, I created an A-list of my own. In fairly short order, I became a West Side society host. My gated, hilltop home furnished the dramatic backdrop for spectacular parties of a hundred or more at a time, typically seated in intimate, conversational groups beside my Olympic-sized swimming pool. Among the regular attendees were such luminaries as Ashley Montagu, Laura (Mrs. Aldous) Huxley, Eddie Albert, and Norman Cousins, and, always, there were glittering constellations of beautiful young women.

On one occasion, Norman turned to me and whispered, "Mani, you must've invited every pretty girl within a ten-mile radius!" Indeed, I had done my best to gather beneath my party umbrellas the brightest stars of the local firmament, the better to assert that I, too, had a place in this glowing sector of the galaxy.

It was during this high-flying period of my life that I met, on separate occasions, two American presidents: Reagan and Clinton. In observing these two very different men in social settings, I noticed a common trait, one that I'd also seen in Gandhi. It might be described as a kind of gracious detachment, as if only a designated portion of their attention could be spared for the occasion at hand, while the rest was reserved for the weighty matters filling other compartments of their minds, matters far removed from the shrimp cocktail.

I wonder whether powerful leaders are not driven by necessity to develop a sort of "extended intelligence" in order to manage their multitude of concerns. I can't say whether any of these presidents ever practiced deep meditation (though I am sure they prayed often), but consciously or not, each may have employed a type of coherent will similar to that which will be discussed in the final chapter of this book.

It was also during this period of champagne and celebrity that a film crew briefly commandeered the master bath of my Bel Air mansion in order to shoot a commercial that featured actress Eva Gabor — soon to be another frequent guest at my soirees — reclining in decadent splendor in a bubble bath. It was not a performance that taxed Eva's dramatic skills, but the director insisted on take after take in order to get the body language right, and I, as master of the house, had certain on-set privileges.

At one point between takes, her eyes found mine, and the ensuing attraction led to a dizzying relationship that took me to the edge of myself — and nearly over it. Later, when asked where we'd met, she would coyly reply, "In his bathtub, dah-ling."

When we began our affair, Eva was known to the world not only as one of the glamorous Gabor sisters, but also as the sweet, spoiled, and somewhat intellectually undernourished character she portrayed on the television series

Green Acres ("Dah-ling, I love you, but give me Park Avenue!"). In stark contrast to the flighty diva she played as a comedienne, Eva was a whip smart businesswoman with a sharp eye for investments, a connoisseur of fine art, and an inspired hostess. She did, however, share one quality with her TV persona. She was a world-class bon vivant, a lover of the finest that money could buy, and her world-class tastes whet my own appetite for luxury. If I'd searched the world over, perhaps I could not have found a woman whose lifestyle represented a greater departure from my roots.

Nonetheless, I dove eagerly into the bubble bath of extravagance and did not surface for some time.

We were high-fliers, and we indulged ourselves ceaselessly. In glorious binges of excess, we savored beluga caviar, Cristal champagne, Belgian truffles, and — above all pleasures — each other. She quickly took over the management of my social calendar, cooing, "Now you have a new secretary, darling!" Her connections increased the candlepower of my poolside gatherings, and she introduced me to Gregory Peck, Tony Curtis, Johnny Carson, and Neil Diamond, among others. As if in surreal caricature of the ongoing spectacle, the booming voice of TV host Robin Leach profiled my rags-to-riches story on *Lifestyles of the Rich and Famous.* I don't know what Gandhi would have made of it all, but I confess that I never washed a dish or thought of goat's milk as anything other than an ingredient in the finest cheeses.

For many newly wealthy people, there is a point on the road of good fortune where acquisition becomes compulsion, and compulsion leads to a kind of sickness of the spirit. The classic film *Citizen Kane* offers a (thinly) fictionalized portrayal of the life of newspaper magnate William Randolph Hearst, whose extravagantly opulent San Simeon estate on the mid-California coast is visited by thousands each year.

In the film, Kane slowly drowns in his own excess until the light of noble ambition that once shone in his eyes is finally extinguished. He can never acquire enough Classical or Renaissance artworks, Venetian furniture, exotic animals, or fine automobiles, because each beautiful thing purchased demands another as a hedge against the fear of losing it, that is perhaps — in truth — the fear that behind all the fine draperies: there is no longer anybody home.

In the final months of my long ride on the merry-go-round with Eva, I began to feel acute vertigo. I had filled six dream houses with fine art and designer furniture, but it all seemed to belong to someone who was not me. Likewise, the shy man photographed with the glamorous blonde at his side was a man I no longer recognized. I adored Eva in private. At the door of my Malibu house, she checked her movie star mask and became the sweet, flirtatious companion every man longs for. But in public, where she shone the brightest, I felt increasingly dim. As the paparazzi showered her with light, I faded. One day, perhaps, I would not have showed up in the photograph at all.

My crisis was both spiritual and psychological, and in the heat of genuine crisis, I think there is little distinction between the two. Like an astronaut propelled far beyond both the gravity and the sight of his home planet, I suddenly found myself without bearings. My life — not the things in it but the ceaseless pursuit of them — had become the very stuff that the Vedas call maya, and I had attached myself to this illusion beyond all measure of spiritual health. It was not exactly guilt that I felt. What I felt was the betrayal of myself. And the greatest betrayal was that, though still a scientist by vocation, I had abandoned the lonely search for truth that makes a scientist worthy of the name.

In my beach house, or when Eva and I managed to slip unnoticed into a concert at the Hollywood Bowl or walk through the galleries of Florentine art at the Los Angeles County Museum, my anxiety would ebb, and we'd briefly find oneness as a couple in love. Like some sultan of old, I almost wished I could make her captive in my tower. But her nature demanded the limelight, while my desire was increasingly to run from it. I began to feel confined by her public, and the more space I sought, the more jealous she became of my freedom. We became as possessive of one another as we were of the pretty things we owned. You know that the best part of a relationship is over when even a drive to the all-night grocery demands an explanation.

One day, probably in an effort to recapture the intimacy of earlier days, she asked me to join her on a cruise. "Darling," she said, "the ship will take us to all those romantic places we've dreamed of seeing together." She painted a delightful picture, and I was tempted to step into it, but I knew that no cruise with Eva could ever truly be just the two of us. With a lump in my throat, I demurred, and in that same sliver of time, our relationship dimmed. I'd come to see that her very public world would never afford the solitude a scientist required, and though she nodded her head in understanding, I'm not certain she could imagine any sane person wanting to get off the merry-go-round.

I consider myself fortunate to have gotten off without serious damage to my emotional health, for I had gone far from my center. Psychologists write of patients who develop elaborate false selves to deal with an outside world that is alien to their nature and to be what that world — and, to some degree, their own egos — want them to be. The false self navigates the world of appearances, often quite deftly, but the spirit can shrivel from lack of sunlight.

It is a testament to the influence of people like Gandhi and Matangini that I avoided both the analyst's couch and the pharmacy, neither of which would really have solved my problem. One day, doctors may exist who can diagnose psychospiritual maladies as adroitly as physicians can spot cancers and psychiatrists can identify depression, but it may require that science and religion work together to develop a new model of the self.

My life in the fast lane did not just suddenly grind to a halt. I had been hurtling along at a pretty rapid clip, and Newton's law of inertia still applied. There remained social obligations to meet, and it took some time to unload all the excess baggage I had accumulated. But in the aftermath of my breakup with Eva, there was indeed a ringing silence on the grounds of my Moraga Place estate in Bel Air, a silence that held an element of sadness. The tables that had only recently seated the rich and powerful were now mostly pushed off to the side; the parties, when I did have them, were smaller and less boisterous. Once I'd deluded myself that the party crowd came for me, but the party crowd comes for other reasons: food, drink, networking, and, most of all, for the affirmation of being seen in the company of success and money, commodities that possess an almost magical potency in Los Angeles.

America had recognized me, actualized me, made me rich, and for a time I saw this as an antidote for the invisibility of being dirt poor in a poor country. I had even wondered whether the endless rituals and provincial superstition of India were not, indeed, sops for ignorance and despair. But every culture has its traps. In America, bank balance takes the place of birth caste. There is a certain dizzy freedom in this, as many enterprising immigrants have found, but there is also a risk. The man with a fortune can come to think himself the better of others, and conversely, his fortune can make even his equals feel lesser.

As a result of the "I want" choices we make throughout our lives, choices that seem smart or exigent at the time, we often become identified with the objects of our desire. In the eyes of others, we become our careers, our marriages, even the cars we drive. This kind of social typology is deeply ingrained in our nature; the King is the King (Heaven forbid he should prove fallible), Mother is Mother (Heaven forbid she should drink or swear), and an accountant is, alas, merely an accountant (God forbid he should dance).

When I stepped back from my decade-long party and took stock of my life, I found that a number of people I had considered close friends had grown distant, and it took some soul-searching to see the reason. In their eyes, I had become my wealth, my lifestyle, even my house! (It was not uncommon to hear people say, "Oh, you know Mani Bhaumik; he's the one with the beautiful palace in Bel Air.") For some who had known me before my gold rush, the adjustment to Mani the millionaire was simply too hard to make. My world was no longer one in which they felt they belonged.

Had Gandhiji been at my side during my meteoric rise to the top of the social ladder, he no doubt would have been whispering in my ear over the tinkling of champagne glasses and the effusive flattery, "Happiness is an inside job, Mani. It can never come from without." As it was, I had to discover this for myself, and not a moment too soon. Unless you have experienced it, you cannot imagine how unhappy a wealthy man can be.

As I stood beside my empty pool on that breezy night more than ten years ago — asking, "Is that all there is?" — the prognosis for my spirit's full recovery was less than certain. I was determined, however, to bring the same zeal to its restoration that I had to making my fortune.

In the back of my mind, there remained the memory of the exaltation I'd felt during my first genuine meditative experience, and how afterward my laser research had seemed more focused and coherent. Something had happened, something unquantifiable. I had slipped into the well of my own being and emerged replenished. Was it possible that a combination of deep meditation and re-immersion in science could yield not only information, but understanding? Could meditation be used as an investigative tool, and its observations affirmed? Tantalizing hints were to be found in the sacred texts of my ancestors, but I sensed a solution lay more broadly in two realms that are equally foreign to most of us: the physical realm of unseen reality revealed by the new physics, and the spiritual realm of mystic experiences.

Perhaps the greatest difference between mysticism — primarily associated with the East — and classical Western science is that mystics make no effort to "atomize" reality, to break it down into analyzable parts. It is perceived as a unity. The Western approach has been very helpful in understanding how things work, but it has not been inordinately concerned with why they work. With the advent of quantum physics and its exotic corollaries, East and West have moved closer, to the point where an eminent physicist like David Bohm can describe material reality as a holomovement.

We will proceed shortly to look at how the view of Western science has changed in just the last few decades to reflect something closer to the deep science implicit in the world's great spiritual traditions. As I woke from my long slumber to behold the startling, sometimes bizarre assertions of modern physics, I saw that many of my colleagues had begun to grapple with the nature of reality in a way that is at least tangentially mystical. Science was tiptoeing to the threshold of spirituality.

I had taken the long way around to rejoin the path I'd chosen in my tenth year, but for me — a boy who'd been rejected for having no prospects — it was a necessary detour. Few men who are less than saints can accomplish much in the world until assured of their worth, and few things are as outwardly affirming of this as success and the love of a beautiful woman. It's true enough to say that I owe a great deal to a blonde in a bubble bath!

I had reached a turning point in my life, where material abundance and ceaseless excitement could no longer hold off the question I had been dying to ask since my boyhood: Could science, in some manner, vouch for the existence of the One whose singularity seemed to anchor all great faiths, and whose presence I had felt so keenly as a young man with his eyes on the dome of night? Could science restore God to those starry skies?

The answer was not one I could hope to find entirely on my own. Notwithstanding male pride, when one has been lost for a while, it is usually a good idea to stop and ask for directions. To navigate my path successfully, I would need to turn for guidance not only to those sources of greater wisdom closest to me, but ultimately to the source of all wisdom. As with all successes worth having, it was not to come overnight.

12

Turning to the Source

I BEGAN, during this introspective period, to explore the common elements of the world's great religions. It struck me that knowledge had probably developed much as a living organism does, branching off endlessly from a primal seed, and that science (more precisely, scientism), in excluding God from its calculus, had cut off its roots.

Like an epidemiologist searching for the carrier of a virus or a detective trying to identify a common M.O. in a series of crimes, I would look for spiritual links in the manner of a scientific sleuth. But even the great Sherlock Holmes might have run into a blind alley if not for those allies (including Dr. Watson) who offered him guidance and clues. The loss of lifelong friendships to which I alluded earlier might have handicapped my quest had it not been for the restorative influence and steadfast presence in my life of three remarkable new friends.

Eddie Albert, the great vaudevillian and comic actor who had, oddly enough, portrayed Eva's determined husband on *Green Acres,* remained my good friend long after the party lights had dimmed. I was introduced to Eddie, not by a talent agent or another Hollywood star, but by

Deepak Chopra, the hugely successful author and spokesman for the Human Potential Movement. Chopra had held
the West Coast release party for his book *Quantum Healing* in my Moraga Place mansion, and soon after, his
friend Eddie Albert and I discovered a kinship in laughter, trust, and a determination to stay light on our feet.
Eddie's sense of humor leavened my sober nature and, as
we shall soon see, laughter has healing and antidepressant
properties that can go far beyond the advertised effects of
Prozac.

The late, great Ashley Montagu was an advocate for
love in an era of abiding hatred. Anthropologist, social scientist, prolific author, and educator, he was arguably the
social conscience of a generation. Ashley may have done
more than any other man of his time to dispel lingering and
pernicious nineteenth-century notions about racial differences. His masterful book *The Fallacy of Race,* published
in 1942, strongly influenced the U.S. Supreme Court's
historic *Brown v. Board of Education* decision, which provided legal fuel for the great civil rights movement of the
'50s and '60s. *The Natural Superiority of Women* (1953),
needless to say, had a profound impact on modern fem-
inism, and *The Elephant Man* (1971), upon which the
play and later film were based, forever altered our perceptions of people with physical disabilities. Considered
by many to be an heir to Darwin, he drew a critical distinction by arguing that evolution was a dynamic process
involving interaction between experience and genetics: we
are participants in our social and biological destinies.

Apart from his astonishing résumé, Ashley was the epitome of British erudition and wit and an advocate of "growing young," that is, maintaining intellectual curiosity even into one's later years. One of his characteristic quotes was, "We should die 'young' . . . but as late as possible." I met him in the mid-1980s, in the company of Laura Huxley, widow of another British prodigy, Aldous Huxley. Ashley and I became close friends, and he encouraged me to write this book. In fact, he wanted to do it jointly, but by then Ashley was not long for this world. In spite of his years, he remained an elegant and vital presence until the day he died, and I am quite certain that he exited this life as youthfully as he had entered it.

I have mentioned that I was lucky to get through my own dark night of the soul without need of psychoanalysis or happy pills, but this was not solely a product of my unassisted will. I had a guardian angel. Of the three men who helped me turn my life around, none had a greater personal impact than Norman Cousins, the great humanist and healer. Sadly, Norman has also passed on, but many who lived through the last three decades of the twentieth century will recall his eternally optimistic face, and even those too young to remember him can feel the influence of his life's work, for Norman was undoubtedly a founding father of what has become known as the holistic health movement, a movement that has now entered the mainstream of medicine.

As with Eddie Albert and Ashley Montagu, I met Norman about 1986, when my social life was at its peak. He'd already been a personage for some time: a long-time editor of the *Saturday Review,* a confidante of Indian Prime Minister Nehru, a Nobel Peace Prize nominee, and, through the United World Federalists Association, an ardent spokesman for international law. But his broader fame stemmed from the remarkable experiences he'd had when, as a younger man, he had been diagnosed with a degenerative cell disease and from the account he lived to write about it, *Anatomy of an Illness as Perceived by the Patient* (1979). This book, and the revolution in self-healing it fostered, ushered in the new field of psychoneuroimmunology (PNI) and earned Norman honorary MD degrees and a clinic in his name at UCLA Medical Center.

Perhaps you have seen the movie *Patch Adams,* in which Robin Williams portrays a pediatric oncologist who attempts, against his peers' fierce resistance, to treat terminally ill children with laughter therapy. Although this character is not based on Norman Cousins, the film seems much influenced by Norman's legacy, for the profoundly simple revelation of his best-selling book is that laughter, along with a course of positive visualization, heals. When Norman was told that his condition was terminal, he promptly checked himself out of the hospital and into a small hotel room, where for weeks he treated himself with a course of funny movies and deep belly laughs. Miraculously (and the word seems justified), his incurable disease went into complete remission, and a new field of medical science was born.

If you have not heard this story before or seen the clinical evidence of its truth, you may be inclined to dismiss it as coincidental, incredible, or a bunch of New Age claptrap. It is none of these. Norman Cousins, colleague of world statesmen, writers, and intellectuals, showed repeatedly that the body's immune cell count can be bolstered by conscious efforts and spontaneous remission can occur by visualizations focused on the afflicted area. PNI is now validating this experimentally. He was walking proof of the influence of mind over matter, and I can testify as one who knows, for until I learned his techniques, I'd suffered frequent colds.

An amusing and instructive anecdote involves Norman's dialogue with Prime Minister Nehru about an efficacious and noninvasive method of controlling the exploding population of India. It is known that the male sperm cell is potent only when the testis remains below a certain temperature (one of the reasons aspiring fathers are advised against wearing tight underwear). Norman demonstrated to Nehru, while holding a thermometer between thumb and forefinger that he could, through mental effort, increase his body temperature in selected areas by a few critical degrees, and this became one of his best-known "proofs."

But Norman Cousins did not stop at self-healing. He sought to extend his techniques to the condition of the world at large. Like Gandhi and Martin Luther King, he was a tiger for peace in history's most violent century. "War is an invention of the human mind," he said, in *Who Speaks for Man?* (1953). "The human mind can invent peace with justice."

His efforts were instrumental in leading to the 1963 Nuclear Test Ban Treaty that President Kennedy negotiated with the Soviets, and he was a champion for the so-called Non-Aligned Nations, India among them. When you see bumper stickers that read Visualize World Peace or Think Globally, Act Locally, think Norman Cousins. But above all else, he was a believer in the limitlessness of human potential and the primacy of consciousness. "Human beings are not locked into fixed limitations," he said, expressing a credo I have lived by.

Life is filled with exquisite symmetries, and if you look for them, life is also filled with invisible silken threads with which, like the spider, we fashion our own webs. These three men — Norman Cousins, offering his own body as

Mani and Norman Cousins at the mansion.

evidence that consciousness alters material reality; Ashley Montagu, employing his first-rate mind to argue that social cooperation and love are critical "selectional factors in human evolution"; and Eddie Albert, the everyman mystic whose humor kept me out of the darker waters of introspection — each, in his own way, echoed the lessons I had learned from Mohandas Gandhi and passionately reaffirmed his assertion that we become what we think.

The missing link between the natural mysticism of my youth and the synthesis I now sought as a scientist, well seasoned by life, was an empirical validation of my belief in the one source of creation. The time had come for me to inquire whether there was a basis for this belief at the nucleus of all the great revealed religions: Hinduism, Buddhism, Judaism, Christianity, and Islam. The time had come to ask — with science itself moving ever closer to the heart of the matter — do we still need God?

My three wise men encouraged me to pursue this quixotic line of inquiry, and if I may share a very personal realization with you, they also opened their hearts to the question that my own father had refused to honor on that starry night so many years before. Perhaps, long before my journey's end, I had already found at least one thing I'd been missing all my life.

13

Code Name "God"

THEOLOGIANS don't much like it when we attempt to peel away the accretions of myth, history, dogma, and sacrament that cloud the origins of their chosen faith. They are liable to accuse us of syncretism, the effort to combine all religions into one, and for the orthodox that is as anathema as the idea of world government is to the extreme political right. When we seek common threads among the world's spiritual doctrines, we may be chided for taking a cafeteria approach to religion: a little from this one, a little from that one, as if we were downloading only our favorite songs from the Internet in order to make up our own "Best of" CD.

It is true enough that some New Age belief systems do little more than dabble in devotion, backing off quickly whenever spiritual discipline becomes too incompatible with one's lifestyle. One cannot really be a part-time Buddhist any more than a self-described Christian can purchase salvation with one hour a week in church. But the irrefutable truth is that at the heart of each of the great religious traditions are three small words: God is One.

In earlier chapters, we introduced some of the tenets of my ancestral religion, Hinduism, and we needn't recap them here. Let's look at a few of the other major religions of the world. Buddhism also sprouted from Indian soil, the brainchild of a pensive young prince whose family reigned in a section of what is now Nepal. His name was Siddhartha Gautama, and he lived in the sixth century BCE. He became the Buddha after forsaking a life of ease to seek out the cause of the human suffering he glimpsed beyond the palace walls. For many centuries, Buddhism supplanted Hinduism as the principal religion of India, spreading into China and Greater Asia, where it remains rooted today.

The Buddha's prescription for pain was deceptively simple: One must free oneself from desire and pursue "right consciousness" through meditation and an awareness of the "oneness" of all creation. Some have speculated that Jesus' teachings were influenced by Buddhist thoughts, though expressed in the less abstract language of Judaism. India ultimately foreswore Buddhism on the grounds that its austere language made no room for a transcendent God, but this very fact has increased its appeal to those Westerners soured on organized religion and has made its tenets compatible with new physics.

If Buddhism finds little dispute with modern science, Taoism, as eloquently postulated by Fritjof Capra in *The Tao of Physics,* might almost be described as a spiritual analog of quantum physics. Elucidated in the *Tao Te Ching* by Lao-tzu, a sixth-century BCE contemporary of Confucius, Taoism urges alignment with a Way (the Tao) that flows ultimately from the unity of opposites (yin-yang) at the heart of nature. Taoism, in contrast to the ethical monotheism of Judaism, Christianity, and Islam, is as much a way of seeing as a way of being, for the Tao (pronounced "dow"), the Way, is the very fabric of the universe, the "self so" order that underlies all. "He who conforms to the Tao," wrote Huai Nan Tzu in the second century BCE, "following the natural processes of heaven and earth, finds it easy to manage the whole world."

Chinese philosophy anticipated the Big Bang theory by insisting that everything sprang from emptiness, or the void. Creation occurs from nothing. As difficult as this is to conceive, the observations of modern science bear out the words written by Lama Anagarika Govinda in his *Foundations of Tibetan Mysticism:* "The relationship of form and emptiness cannot be conceived as a state of mutually exclusive opposites, but only as two aspects of the same reality that co-exist and are in continual cooperation." We will see later how closely this statement corresponds to the aforementioned David Bohm's notions of explicate and implicate orders of existence.

Zen, which developed in China and was introduced to Japan around 1200 CE, abstracts Buddhism even further, aiming toward enlightenment through a practiced attention to mind and mindfulness. *Satori* (enlightenment) is achieved by "pointing directly to the human mind, seeing into one's own nature, and attaining Buddhahood." Truth and happiness are to be found in attending with devotion to the matters of everyday life, such as gardening or making tea, because all things are a manifestation of nature's essential and undivided oneness. Similarly, we shall see that the building blocks of material reality are in fact only excitations of the underlying abstract continuum. In the whimsically (sometimes maddeningly) mind-teasing parlance of Zen, "God is a no-thing" but that does not mean that God is nothing. It means that God is not a thing.

The central discipline of Zen is *zazen* (sitting meditation), which is practiced for hours at a time in the usually remote and sublimely peaceful monasteries. Again, the emphasis is on relaxed attention, a "coherent consciousness" by which the mind is tuned in to the presence of the infinite, eternal One, as if all other noises but the soft buzzing of the cosmic hive had ceased. If this sounds almost preciously abstract, be "mindful" of this: Modern physics suggests that when we penetrate the subatomic levels of reality down through the very fabric of space, we will find that everything is interconnected. Long before David Bohm and Basil Hiley, Zen monks intuited this interconnectedness. Could the reason be that the connection lay in consciousness itself? With that, I will leave you a moment to contemplate the sound of one hand clapping!

Before turning to the Western traditions, it should be acknowledged that many people of Judeo-Christian background have difficulty with the "negative" element in Asian religion. Words like emptiness, nothingness, and void conjure bleak pictures; the idea that behind the entire world's plenitude is a "no-thing" — let alone that we'd want to join with it — can be a bit unsettling. Paradoxically (and the essence of both mysticism and quantum physics is paradox), what is perceived as empty can also be perceived as full, in the sense of an infinite potential. Zero, as we shall see, implies more than nothing.

An ancient bridge between East and West is the doctrine of the Gnostics, a varied group of nominally Christian thinkers and mystics whose influence was felt most strongly in the first and second centuries CE. The Gnostics identified the First Cause — the true God — as residing in the Pleroma (the Fullness), beyond space, time, and causation, while material reality is a kind of counterfeit, the creation of lesser gods. (See the *Matrix* films for a comic book popularization of this idea.) Branded as heretics for questioning the Catholic clergy's authority and for their belief that an immanent "God spark" remained even in Fallen Man (thereby eliminating the need for redemption from Original Sin), the Gnostics moved underground and later fed the roots of both Protestantism and Theosophy.

Gnosticism shared much with the philosophy of Neo-Platonism, which postulated a higher dimensional realm of ideal forms whose source is the One and whose shadows are what we mistake for reality. The most famous depiction of this way of seeing the world is Plato's analogy of the cave. He suggested that we (humankind) sit facing the blank wall of the cave in which we dwell, like children waiting for a puppet show. Behind us — where we dare not venture — is the cave entrance, guarded by a fire circle that keeps intruders out and us in. From time to time, an object from the outside world passes between the fire and the cave opening, and its shadow is briefly thrown against the wall. We applaud, for this projection is our only reality.

From the spiritual matrix of apocalyptic Judaism, Hellenistic philosophy, and Near Eastern death and resurrection myth sprang the great and world-altering message of Christianity, embodied by a messenger who taught us to "Love thy neighbor as thyself" and so much believed in his oneness with God that he went willingly to the cross. Nothing in Jesus' teachings conflicts with the essential tenets or mystical foundations of the other world religions, which is one reason he is revered by them all. "The Kingdom of Heaven is within" is a perfectly cogent statement of the fact that we are all participants in the great concert of creation, that the macrocosm is the microcosm, and that we are connected to one another and to the source of all being — the "I am that I am" of Exodus, the One of the Neo-Platonists.

Judaism and Islam, so tragically at odds (as only brothers can be), are both heirs to Abraham's fervent monotheism. While Judaism hailed Yahweh as the one God long before Christ, the Islamic counterpart, Allah, awaited Mohammed's prophecies in the seventh century CE. Mohammed hailed Jesus as a great prophet but felt that Christianity had become decadent and had forgotten its source in "the Book" (that is, the word of God). Therefore, Allah's word needed to be reinscribed as the Koran. But it only compounds the tragedy to think that Allah — simply the Arabic word for God — is of a different fabric from Yahweh or Brahman or the Tao. The Islamic creed, "There is no God but Allah (God)" states the obvious: God is One.

The common ground of all these great faiths is to be found in their essence: mystical insight. Insight, by its nature, is experiential. It cannot be effectively taught, or preached, or read about, except by way of analogy, allegory, or, most clumsily, dogma. But the testimony of the mystics seems eminently convincing. Whether one is a Christian quietist, a Jewish Kabbalist, a Muslim Sufi, a Hindu yogi, a Buddhist Tantrist, or a Zen master, when you get down to the level of religious epiphany, the experience is the same: *dissolution of ego boundaries, a merging of the observer and the observed, a union with the one source of all.* Contrary to the scientific bias that mysticism is a vague, metaphysical thing, the mystical experience itself is evidently of great clarity; otherwise, how could so many from such diverse backgrounds describe it in such similar terms?

The majority of scientists still cringe at the mere mention of mysticism, yet they are, as it were, backing into the cosmic sea. You might assume that I am predisposed to a transcendental outlook, as I was born and raised in a deeply spiritual environment. But I am a scientist first, and scientists are skeptical creatures. I had to do a lot of questioning before I was able to reconcile the two aspects of my nature. The answers I found may surprise you as much as they did me.

In the following chapters, we will uncover — through a quick dip into quantum physics — that when we penetrate to the deepest level of reality, we seem to find an undivided totality, an "emptiness" that is — paradoxically — full. The more we learn, the clearer it becomes that the precepts of mysticism differ from those of modern physics mostly in language and methodology. Could it be that the common experience of the mystics has an analog in the "unbroken wholeness" of the quantum physicists?

By far the greatest obstacle to reconciling science and spirituality has been the personification of God. The prophets and priests of all global religions have historically offered their followers wide latitude in their depiction of the Almighty, whether that depiction is a stern patriarch with a white beard, a serpent-tongued she-demon, or an elephant. They have realized that we have tremendous difficulty conceptualizing, let alone believing in, things beyond the pale of our own senses, and they have traditionally kept the "secret" for themselves, the secret being that God is abstract and not a person or symbol that people might worship. But at some point, even the priests fell prey to their own sleight-of-hand and began to believe their own press, just as the mathematicians — no less of a priesthood — have too often mistaken their elegant equations for the truths they represent.

Einstein remarked that science grew out of the refinement of our daily thinking. In its infancy, science was a close cousin of philosophy. Newton's *Principia,* considered to be the first great scientific text, bears the title, *The Mathematical Principles of Natural Philosophy.* But ever since relativity theory and quantum physics described a reality strikingly at odds with our perception, physics increasingly has become the province of mathematicians. This is because math furnishes the only vocabulary capable of precisely describing this reality. Naturally, this has driven even many highly educated people away from science.

I will not ask you to master the rudiments of this vocabulary, nor even to solve a single equation, but I will ask that you accompany me in the next few chapters on a guided tour through the strange landscape of modern science. You have every reason to ask why you should do so, and the answer is as dramatically straightforward as the Zen master's answer to his pupil: because my own experience has shown me that it is the only way to appreciate the reconciliation of the scientific and spiritual worldviews. The reward for this effort, I think I can assure you, will be a life enriched and experienced more fully.

If I may offer one aide for navigating in the remarkable "space" we are about to enter, it is this: While you're here, try to relax your mental fix on the image of God that has been most familiar to you since childhood. Let it slip to the back of your mind; you can always reclaim it later (and that is perfectly all right). It isn't required that you do this, but it will help, and you may be surprised by what new visions come bubbling up from inside.

14

The Loom of Heaven

AMERICA'S FOUNDING FATHERS were men of both science and faith who attributed creation to "the Laws of Nature and Nature's God." Not the Christian God or the Jewish God or the Islamic God: Nature's God. In that hallowed tradition epitomized in the Declaration of Independence, I am strongly inclined to believe: A clear-eyed appraisal of the warp and weft of physical reality reveals that woven throughout the universe is an abstract intelligence, which we may, without offense to either science or religion, be permitted to call divine.

Cosmology, which explores the evolution of the universe, has revealed such sublime order in the design of the physical world that it often seems to suggest the hand of a single architect. And indeed, the elegant symmetries and incredible precision of universal laws do argue for some kind of governing force, a higher order of reality. Before we try, however, to cozy up to a power so mind-bogglingly abstract, we'd better take a step back and look at how science has come to view physical reality in the wake of the revolution brought about by relativity and quantum physics.

From the moment we are introduced as high school students to the molecular and atomic structure of material things, we know that reality is not always what it seems. When we drink a glass of water, we are not aware of the trillion trillion water molecules coursing down our throats, much less of the two hydrogen and one oxygen atoms that make up each molecule. With each breath we take, we inhale about a billion trillion molecules, and yet we do not gag. Such examples, where we hardly recognize what's just under the facade of our daily world, are to be found everywhere throughout the universe.

It is always easier to understand something if we have a model, and a good way to understand the material world is to think of it as consisting of three layers. They are not so much like the neatly stacked layers of a cake as like the layers of pigment on a painter's canvas, each seen through the others and all forming the impression of "one color." As they all interpenetrate, the division into three is somewhat arbitrary, but visualizing it this way helps greatly in understanding how matter comes to be.

The first layer of reality is the observable universe of material objects and natural phenomena that surrounds us and with which we interact through our five primary senses. This is the reality that has a *thereness* (that is, it seems to exist outside of us), which led Descartes and his followers to presume that there was an irreconcilable split between mind and matter — between the perceiver and the perceived. That is the only reality for most people. As marvelous as this first layer is to behold, however, it is merely the tip of the iceberg.

The second layer of reality requires a leap in imagination. It is characterized by a ceaseless interplay of energy at a microscopic scale, at an unimaginably fast rate, a level that our senses are not equipped to perceive. If evolution did not condition us this way, we would all suffer intolerable vertigo.

We are outfitted to comprehend matter in its "packaged" form, but not with X-ray vision to see what's inside. The only way to look inside the wrapping is with tools of detection that extend the capability of our senses, tools that include not only electron microscopes and particle accelerators but some rather intricate mathematical constructs as well.

The idea that everything is made of atoms goes all the way back to the Greek philosopher Democritus. And what exactly is an atom made of? It consists of a positively charged nucleus in which protons and neutrons are bound together, balanced by the negatively charged electrons surrounding it. The protons and neutrons, in turn, are made of even tinier particles called quarks. All the matter that makes up our everyday world is composed of two kinds of fundamental particles—quarks and electrons.

Thanks to Einstein, we now know that quarks and other elementary particles are nothing but discrete packets of energy. Although the objects in our midst appear as solid and substantial as the Rock of Gibraltar, their constituent parts are in a constant state of flux. The engine of this flux is energy, and its top speed is the speed of light.

No one, including physicists, knows exactly what energy is, but it reveals itself to us through the forms it takes. We can measure the surge through an electrical circuit or observe the explosion that results from a chemical reaction; we can feel the heat energy of the sun's nuclear alchemy or thrill to the kinetic energy of g-forces produced by a roller coaster. The names given to these forms of energy are artificial distinctions that make it easier for us to get a handle on what we cannot see; there is only *energy* doing work of different kinds.

But how is energy stabilized into quarks and electrons, let alone the complicated structures we recognize as rocks, trees, birds, you, and me? If all things are made of this abstract and chimerical substance known as energy, why do we see them as stable and unchanging? Why don't the fundamental particles simply fall apart? Because their energy is confined, like a genie in the bottle — but these bottles are not physical. They are what are known as fields, and I'll warn you in advance, these are really abstract. Now we are on the brink of the third layer of reality.

The fields are known to us by way of the forces associated with them. Take, for instance, the field that most palpably affects our daily existence: the gravitational field. We can neither see nor touch it. We go about our day-to-day activities without even giving its existence a thought. Yet it is demonstrably real. We feel it when we jump, and we rely upon it whenever we throw a ball into the air, confident that gravity will bring it back.

It was Isaac Newton (with a debt to both Galileo and Kepler) who first formally identified gravity as an invisible force capable of acting across great distances upon objects as large as planets or as small as croquet balls. The thinking of his time, however, was so mechanistic that Newton failed to see gravity for what it was, and essentially he walked away in puzzlement. How could something as nonmaterial as force affect something physical without a connective medium? How could a thing be moved without being touched?

The first glimmering of a phenomenon that could operate without direct contact, an influence that could pervade an entire region of space, came in the early part of the nineteenth century, when English physicist Michael Faraday moved a magnet within a coil and produced electrical current.

Faraday, unlike Newton, did not know enough to get it wrong. Nearly a century later, Albert Einstein, another academic underachiever with the gift of genius, mused about whether Faraday would have hit upon the notion of a field if he had not been a high school dropout! Although there was no material link between a magnet and a coil, Faraday perceived that magnetism, a nonmaterial entity, was inducing current in the coil, and the concept of a field was christened.

Although it may seem obvious to us now that these two ostensibly separate forces — electricity and magnetism — are closely related, it wasn't until the middle of the nineteenth century that James Clerk Maxwell united them as electromagnetism and further proposed that light itself was one of its forms. In Maxwell's groundbreaking equations, electromagnetism manifests itself in waves, a fact experimentally demonstrated by Heinrich Hertz that ushered in the age of mass communication through broadcast media.

But Maxwell, like Newton before him, was still convinced that electromagnetic waves could only be propagated through some material medium. For more than two millennia, that medium was thought to be something called the aether. It took the prodigious intellect of Albert Einstein to recognize that the medium was empty space itself. Furthermore, Einstein showed us that space, time, and field cannot exist separately; they are always magnificently intertwined in their existence. A field is a physical state of space itself, and space does not exist without a field. Reality hasn't been the same since.

The example of inducing electrical current into a coil is a good illustration of a field effect. So is the way that the Earth's magnetic field aligns the needle of a compass on a north-south axis, no matter where we are on the globe. These phenomena meet the basic definition of all fields, which is that they permeate a region of space and can be delineated at each point. This is a difficult, if not impossible, thing to visualize, but it becomes easier the more we are made aware of a particular field's influence.

So far, we have been talking about classical *manifest fields,* those whose influence is felt locally, like our own planet's field of gravity or the way static electricity makes our hair stand up on a dry winter day. We could easily be misled into thinking that an electric field is something that arises from matter, like the heat rising from a car's engine or the way iron filings line up around the poles of a magnet.

But this is not the case; the truth is far stranger. Even if we yank the Earth from the sky, an *unmanifest field* having the blueprint for gravity will still remain in empty space!

These unmanifest fields pervade all space and time, and they are known as quantum fields. The unmanifest field's influence is *nonlocal*, in the sense that it is felt equally in all parts of the universe. Comprehending this intrinsic fundamental reality of our cosmos is a key to grasping our later discussions on how science supports the concept of the *one source*.

How did we come to realize the existence of unmanifest quantum fields? We learn as children that every snowflake that drops from the sky is different, but one of the most mysterious aspects of quantum physics is that elementary particles, such as electrons, are *absolutely* identical everywhere in the universe, no matter when or where they are created. The amount of their mass, electric charge, and spin are always exactly the same.

This mystery of the matching particles was solved in the last half of the twentieth century when physicists determined that underlying quantum fields give birth to elementary particles. A new branch of physics known as quantum field theory was the foundation of this revelation, which takes us to the brink of some very heady mathematics (which we won't address) and some very strange ideas (which we will).

As MIT's Frank Wilczek, one of the high priests of quantum field theory and a newly minted Nobel laureate sums it up, "In quantum field theory, the primary elements of reality are not individual particles, but underlying fields.

Thus, for example, all electrons are but excitations of an underlying field, naturally called the electron field, *which fills all space and time"* (my italics). The same holds true for all the fundamental particles of which matter is made.

To grasp this profound departure from the billiard ball model of atomic theory many of us grew up with, imagine these elementary particles as being like the spray that's thrown up as ocean waves crash against the rocks, only to fall back into the sea from which it came. My world was shaken as a young man with the realization that things I had previously thought of as solid and inert, in fact, consisted of the quantized "lumps of energy," we call fundamental particles.

Now if it sounds like we are talking about the idea of something "virtual" becoming something "real," that is actually what happens. Things get "curiouser and curiouser!" as Alice might say. Are we in Wonderland? It sure appears that way. Strange as it may seem, just like a compulsive credit card addict, a quantum field constantly borrows energy from space, creating pairs of virtual particles (matter and anti-matter), most of which have a life span far, far shorter than that of the ocean spray. The energy debt to space must be repaid, and the larger the debt, the shorter the time to pay back. But as soon as there is sufficient energy surplus made available by any source, stable particles are able to emerge from the quantum field and have a "real" existence in the universe. Without energy there are only virtual particles.

Thinking about virtual particles, physicist Richard Feynman, who shared the Nobel Prize for the quantum field

theory, remarked in jest, "Created and annihilated, created and annihilated — what a waste of time!" But virtual
particles do produce some important effects that can be
measured, giving tangible evidence of the existence of the
numinous quantum fields.

Don't worry too much about terms like quantum or
quantized. A quantum is simply a small, discrete unit in
which a form of energy may express itself. A quantum of
light, for example, is a photon. So, although light, as a
type of electromagnetic radiation, is generally conceived
of in waves, those waves themselves are made up of
quanta, just as the stream of audio and video coming into
your Internet port is made up of bits of data. And unlike
our familiar classical fields, the magnitude of energy of a
quantum field is not continuous but discrete, or quantized.

All of the known quantum fields possess the following
confounding characteristic: They are not, in any geomet-
rical sense, locatable, yet they are everywhere. This is
because, according to Werner Heisenberg's well established uncertainty principle, a quantum field cannot have
a fixed value at any given time, not even the value of zero.
As a result, the amplitude (the size) of a field must change
all the time, producing what are known as vacuum fluctuations. It is a "now you see it, now you don't situation," but
we observe the effect of these fluctuations in the Casimir
Effect and in several other phenomena.

The Casimir Effect sounds like something dreamed up
by a science fiction writer, but it is actually not that esoteric. If you'll allow me a brief detour, I think it may help to
pave the road ahead. In 1948, in order to demonstrate the

effect of vacuum fluctuations of the electromagnetic field, Dutch physicist Hendrick Casimir predicted that *even in a vacuum*, a measurable force will act to push together two parallel metal plates. If this were true, it would indicate that some other form of energy was acting upon the plates, an energy that could exist even in the absence of any familiar force.

Casimir was right, but it was 1996 before physicist Steven Lamoreaux conclusively demonstrated the existence of this electromagnetic ghost force. The notion that all fields fluctuate at the quantum level has now been validated, thus providing our strongest evidence of the actuality of the unmanifest quantum fields themselves.

Along with the constant creation and annihilation of virtual particles, the wild fluctuation of the unmanifest fields creates a quantum frenzy at the microscopic dimensions of space. This behavior gets increasingly more energetic at smaller distance and time scales. Thus, empty space is not empty at all. It is a seething cauldron of quantum activity.

The unmanifest quantum fields interlace throughout the cosmos like multidimensional fabrics woven on a celestial loom, and strangest of all, as we shall see, each infinitesimal weave of the fabric contains, so to speak, the whole cloth, just as the poet William Blake saw "a world in a grain of sand."

Feeling dizzy? Good. Occasional disorientation is the occupational hazard of all truth seekers. Moreover, it shakes us from our normal frame of reference. Before we go on, take a moment to contemplate the new world around you — a world in which there is no such thing as empty space, and the most crucial elements of your existence are things you can't see.

In addition to quarks and electrons, there are a host of other fundamental matter particles, like neutrinos, but they are either unstable or interact very weakly. So we do not observe them except under special circumstances, such as in a high-energy "particle" physics lab. These matter particles are all products of the various matter fields. However, the more familiar force fields also have their respective particles (elementary force particles). For example, a photon is the particle associated with the electromagnetic force field and the graviton is presumed to be the particle related to the gravity force field. In the following chapter we'll consider the remaining force fields and the Holy Grail of physics: the quest for their common origin.

A word about terminology. The fact that we can speak almost interchangeably about fields, on the one hand, and the force and matter they give rise to, on the other, is at the core of the quantum field theory: Both elementary force particles and elementary matter particles are merely excitations of their corresponding underlying fields, which makes the quantum fields, in a sense, the breeding ground of material creation.

The triumph of the quantum field theory in explaining all the observed fundamental particles is a hallmark of twentieth-century physics. Physicists are so convinced of its validity that they have constructed what is known as

the standard model of particle physics, which successfully categorizes the observed fundamental particles in
a manner somewhat similar to the well-known periodic
table of the elements (hydrogen, helium, uranium, and
so on) that we learn in high school. Still, because of its
abstractness and the very esoteric math involved, this
perception-altering theory remains Greek to most of us.

Indeed, the unseen but ubiquitous quantum fields and
their vacuum fluctuations may seem utterly alien, but so
was the idea of radio waves a century ago. Now we readily
accept them as part of reality. In fact, radio communication in all its applications may have been the medium
through which it became possible for nonscientists to con-
ceptualize something as abstract as an invisible "it" that
technology can channel. The omnipresent quantum fields
are yet a further step into a phantom world, but regardless
of our puzzlement, they remain stubbornly and definitely
there, permeating even the darkest sectors of space where
there is no MTV!

15

The Holy Grail of Physics

WHEN SIR GALAHAD of King Arthur's Camelot ventured about in his quest for the Holy Grail, he came afar to a maimed king's land. He found a kingdom in ruins, laid waste by drought, despair, and division, its bedridden king unable to unite his people. Legend has it that in the presence of the injured king Galahad was granted the object of his quest — a transcendent vision of the Grail — that came as the result of asking the right question: "What ails the king and his kingdom?" Once the true nature of things had been acknowledged, the wound was healed, the unity was restored, and the blighted kingdom began to blossom again.

Likewise, in science great leaps in perception often come to us by way of visitors, men and women who, due to their unique perspective, ask the right question at the right time. Albert Einstein was such a visitor, a Grail knight with a shock of white hair and dark pools of wisdom in his eyes. To quote physicist Brian Greene, "Einstein wanted to illuminate the workings of the universe with a clarity never before achieved, allowing us all to stand in awe of its sheer beauty and elegance." The quest that consumed

Einstein's imagination was the quest for the unification of the fields.

Einstein envisioned that the known force fields that control all natural phenomena ought to have a common foundation describable by the tenets of a unified field theory. His belief in a comprehensible and elegantly simple universe was so strong that he devoted the last thirty years of his professional life to it, but unlike Galahad, the object of his quest remained out of reach until recently.

The puzzle that Einstein was not able to solve, but contemporary physicists are coming close to putting together, is this: Why, if everything is ultimately made of one substance — energy — does nature provide so many different types of fields for energy to work its magic? Most physicists are now quite convinced that these diverse fields, including a few that Einstein had not considered, are nothing but different aspects of a single field.

In the previous chapter, we saw how the existence of gravity and electromagnetism explains much of what we observe in the first layer of reality. There are also, however, less familiar but equally crucial force fields that operate only in the tiny world of the subatomic. In order to detect them, we'll have to go, like Alice in Wonderland, from the big to very small.

One of the first logical questions that arises when we talk about the nucleus of an atom is: What keeps those positively charged protons from flying apart? After all, like charges repel. This does not present such a problem when we are looking at the hydrogen atom, which consists of a single positively charged proton and a single negatively charged electron.

But in order to get helium, the nuclei of two hydrogen atoms must be fused, along with two neutrons, and likewise in increasing numbers with all the other atoms. What is the agent of this fusion? What glue could possibly counteract the mutual repulsion of positively charged protons sitting, as it were, side by side? It is the strong nuclear force that binds the nuclei as well as their constituent quarks, and lucky for us, it's a force more than a hundred times stronger than that of electromagnetism and almost unimaginably stronger than the gravitational force that keeps the moon orbiting the earth.

The fourth of the great natural forces, in addition to gravity, electromagnetism and the strong nuclear force, is the weak nuclear force. Befitting its name, it almost always receives the weakest exposure because its range of influence is limited to one thousandth of the size of even the tiny proton. This force governs the rate and process of radioactive decay within the nucleus, and it can be thought of as an essential sidekick to the strong force for making helium from hydrogen in the solar furnace that supplies energy to all life forms on earth. In spite of its unassuming name, the weak nuclear force, or weak force, is still more than a million billion billion billion times stronger than the force of gravity!

Although such disparate strengths of the forces might be difficult to perceive, this variance is responsible for the universe's most desirable features, especially those that give rise to life. For example, if the force of gravity was not extremely weak compared to the other forces, the many atoms of which humans, planets, or stars consist would simply collapse upon each other. In fact, life could not have emerged as it has with even a tiny variation in these strengths. We will be astonished to see, however, what happens to these inequalities under extreme circumstances.

As we've seen, physicist James Clerk Maxwell demonstrated the unification of electric and magnetic force fields, which we have since called the electromagnetic field. It was not until a century later that scientists were able to fully glimpse the existence of the unification of all the forces and fields.

To help explain the unification of forces, we must speak first of nature's *symmetries*. What do we mean by this term? The pillars of the Parthenon demonstrate symmetry along a line. The architecture remains the same even if we exchange one pillar for the other. A golf ball exemplifies a rotational symmetry; regardless of how you turn the ball, it looks the same. When we talk about nature's symmetries, however, we are not talking about things *looking* the same, but about elemental forces and particles giving up their distinguishing "marks" and behaving as if they were characterized by the same natural laws. The forces and fields we know are the result of broken symmetries of nature. So, restoration of symmetries is the magic key to unification, and unification is key to understanding the common source.

In the late 1960s, physicists Steven Weinberg, Abdus Salam, and Sheldon Glashow succeeded in doing for the weak and electromagnetic forces what Maxwell had done with electricity and magnetism in 1873; they showed theoretically that at either very high temperatures or equivalently at very small distances, the distinction between electromagnetism and the weak force simply vanishes. (For reference, the very small distances we are talking about are in the neighborhood of .0000000000000001 centimeter, which is a thousand times smaller than the proton!) At these small distances, some of nature's foundational symmetry is restored, allowing the weak and the electromagnetic forces to behave similarly. The three physicists were awarded the Nobel Prize for their pioneering breakthrough.

In 1983, a research team at CERN in Geneva headed by Carlo Rubia and Simon van der Meer gave conclusive experimental verification of the electroweak unification. Rubia and van der Meer also received Nobel Prizes. Discovery of the unity of such diverse forces has broken the barrier in physicists' minds against the seeming impossibility of the unification of nature. We are getting closer to the common source. Alice, take another sip!

Unification of the strong nuclear force with the electromagnetic and the weak forces would be evident in what physicists call a grand unified theory (GUT, for short). Direct proof of grand unification is unlikely because it is presumed to occur at a scale fourteen orders of magnitude (one followed by fourteen zeros) smaller than the dimension at which electromagnetism joins the weak force. However, recent observation (the oscillation of tiny, ghostlike neutrinos between their various families) is considered to be a very encouraging sign for GUT. Also, the fact that we and everything else in the universe exist due to a slight excess of matter over antimatter in the early universe is believed to require such unification.

Gravity is the stickler and is not easily folded into such a microscopic omelet. But because it is nonetheless primarily a quantum field, gravity is expected to be joined with the rest. Even though a consistent mathematical formulation exhibiting the unification of all the fields is not yet complete, physicists are quite sanguine about its feasibility. Stephen Hawking, for one, thinks so, as do Nobel laureates Steven Weinberg, Murray Gell-Mann, and others.

What gives physicists such confidence is the fact that the strength of interaction of the diverse forces appears to become equal at nature's own dimensions, called the Planck's dimensions, after the genius who conceived of them back in 1899. Planck's length is as small as the universe is large, and certainly smaller than Alice ever got! Let's take a moment to ask how science grasps such an inconceivably tiny space.

We all acknowledge that functioning in our own world requires standardized units of distance, mass (energy), and time. Think of how difficult it would be to give the simplest direction, let alone to build a house, without such references. Now, whether you happen to be a postmodern agnostic who believes the cosmos arose according to some kind of self-generating binary code like that which runs your computer, or a person who glimpses in a butterfly's wing the faint brushstroke of a Creator, isn't it logical to think that nature would require her own standards?

Max Planck believed so, and he derived a set of units of measurements that are the same throughout the universe.

Max Planck calculated the value of nature's units of measurement in terms of our own units, using three universal physical constants: the speed of light in a vacuum, Newton's gravitational constant, and Planck's constant. Newton's gravitational constant explains why your weight on earth is six times more than what it would be on the moon, while Planck's constant determines, among other things, the size of a quantum particle. Planck's dimensions are the coordinates we use to navigate the deepest subatomic realm.

To give an idea of scale, Planck's length is to a single human cell as that cell is to the entire visible universe. In other words, our human cell is in the middle of the largest of the large and the smallest of the small. An element of space has a smallest possible size, which is roughly equal to Planck's unit of length. Therefore, the fabric of space can be envisioned to be constituted of Planck's length.

Although efforts are underway for indirect verifications, we have no way of directly measuring the strength of the forces in Planck's dimensions because it would require a particle accelerator, a kind of physicists' microscope, much larger than the solar system. Obviously, we cannot build such an accelerator, but we can predict the results with some confidence by projecting our laboratory observations. It is a well-proven scientific technique that we test things on a small model to predict their behavior on a larger scale. Airplane builders routinely test small prototypes in wind tunnels before building a jumbo plane and putting a test pilot's life at risk.

Following this tradition, when we extrapolate our laboratory measurements to Planck's dimensions, using the highly successful quantum field theory, the strength of interaction of all the forces becomes equal. Again, according to Wilczek, "From its much inferior strength at accessible energies, gravity ascends to equality with the other interactions at roughly the Planck scale.... *Even in the absence of a detailed theory we find here a concrete, semiquantitative indication that all of the basic forces arise from a common source*" (my italics). Near Planck's scale, the strong force is presumed to be no longer stronger than the electroweak force or that of gravity!

In addition to the basic forces, the common source that Wilczek refers to also includes various matter fields, such as the electron field. The matter fields package energy into fundamental particles, while the force fields use them as building blocks to generate everything. What unifies all those force fields and matter fields to establish the common source Wilczek alludes to? It is presumed to be facilitated by nature's highest possible symmetry, called *supersymmetry,* and at or near the Planck's scale, all the fields are believed to behave as merely different aspects of *one field,* as singular and transcendent as the Grail itself.

The distinctions we make among forms of energy — electrical, mechanical, chemical, heat, and light — are strictly for our convenience. What's important to remember is that they represent only one substance: energy. Similarly, the division of the four forces of nature — gravity, electromagnetism, strong nuclear force and weak nuclear force — is also man-made, in order to facilitate scientific investigation of our daily world. There is no deeper rationale for this division.

Einstein coined the term "unified field theory" for the premise of giving a simple unified foundation of fields. Following that tradition, some physicists dub the common source the unified field, a logical enough label. But this is not a new field in the sense that it has its own distinct fundamental particle. It merely represents the fact that all the fields in our universe are now believed to arise from a common source, which may be appropriately called the *primary field*. Unification is also popularly known under the umbrella of the "theory of everything," and although some scientists may gag on this expression, even the Nobel committee has recently taken to using it.

Could this primary field be embedded in space itself, even though we can not see it? In our day-to-day experience, space is like a stage where events play themselves out. How can the source be encoded there? The very idea defies common sense. Recall however, that Einstein revolutionized our idea of space. He showed that space and time are not absolute, but malleable. Space, which appears to be formless, is actually curved around a heavy mass like a galaxy that literally acts as a giant optical lens. The Hubble space telescope graphically demonstrates this.

Contrary to our notion of space as an idle bystander, space is dynamically involved in everything that happens in the universe. We have already seen that "empty" space is not empty at all. In fact, quantum physics suggests that the primary field, possessing the basic blueprint of all things physical, is encoded in its fabric. Normally, physicists think of unification leading up to the primary field to be possible only at the extraordinarily high temperatures of the infant universe. How, then, can I maintain that this unification exists everywhere even in the space around (and within!) your big toe?

It is because, according to quantum field theory, physics at extremely high temperatures is equivalent to physics at the fundamentally small distances typical of Planck's dimensions. We can perceive this more graphically by recalling our realization that empty space experiences frenetic quantum activity in the microscopic dimensions. And as a further consequence of Heisenberg's famous uncertainty principle, these activities become more energetic as distance and time scales approach the infinitesimal. The quantum frenzy *simulates* by its blurring of distinctions (that is the restoration of symmetries), the high temperatures characteristic of the early universe.

Therefore, the primary field, being present at the very fabric of space, is orchestrating the continuing symphony of our universe. Did it play a role in creation also? Science hints at some striking inferences that we will explore in the next chapter. We will consider the implications of unification and examine the telltale clues the universe has left us about its creation and evolution. These bits of evidence suggest the likely scenario that the primary field, having the plan of the entire universe, unfolded sequentially to create it.

Could it be that nature repeats its pattern in the human genome? Our genome (DNA), which is present in our very first cell and consists of twenty-three pairs of chromosomes, possesses the blueprint of an entire human being. While miraculously putting together about a hundred trillion cells in the right proportion to create the various organs of the human body, the gnome remains ever-present in each one of those cells, administering different aspects of our biological existence. Only a small percentage of the genome is active in an adult cell, and this *expression* oversees the proper functioning of that particular unit. Nevertheless, it possesses instructions for the whole works. This is now vividly demonstrated in cloning, where, for instance, an entire sheep can be replicated from any adult sheep cell.

Presence of a cosmic genome in and throughout the fabric of space is like another modern marvel, the hologram. In an ordinary photograph, each grain of the picture corresponds to a point on the subject. But in a hologram, the *potentiality* of an entire three-dimensional image is encoded in each point of the holographic plate. Even when the plate is shattered, the right kind of light will produce the total picture from a single shard, albeit with some loss of clarity.

If you have tracked the mystery this far, then you are as intrepid a detective as Sherlock Holmes and deserve a look at the best evidence. While gathering the clues, we'll enjoy a cosmic fashion show as the universe puts on, layer by layer, the garments of a reality we can recognize as our own. It is not likely that you will ever look at her quite the same way again.

16

The Unfolding Universe

MORE THAN five thousand feet above Los Angeles and a scant forty-five minutes from downtown, the once-great observatory on Mt. Wilson still stands, in some disrepair and as much a destination for picnickers and hang gliding aficionados as for working astronomers. In the winter months, while the Los Angeles basin suns itself at seventy-eight degrees Fahrenheit, snow falls on the cluster of white domes and in the deep pine forest that surrounds them.

Today, researchers from various universities utilize Mt. Wilson's telescopes retrofitted with adaptive optics to counteract atmospheric disturbances and to minimize the light pollution from the city. Back in the 1920s, however, when an ambitious young astronomer named Edwin Hubble focused the observatory's shining new hundred-inch Hooker telescope to the nebulae, the stars burned brighter than any constellation of city lights. Hubble settled a cosmic question pending since the time of Kant, and found the suspected "island universes" instead to be individual galaxies, some flung to the edge of visibility.

Strange as it seems now, science did not have observational proof before Hubble's time, a mere three-quarters of a century ago, that the universe consisted of more than our Milky Way. Telescopes powerful enough to look clearly beyond it did not exist. With his discovery, coming as it did within a decade of Einstein's proposed model of the universe based on general relativity, the cosmos took an enormous leap in size.

But it was what Hubble and Vesto Slipher discovered when they began to measure the color spectra of these distant new galaxies that made Einstein seem a reluctant prophet and cosmology a nascent branch of science. Einstein, you see, in spite of what his own equations implied, believed along with everyone else at the time that the universe was essentially static. Hubble discovered otherwise.

He found indisputable evidence that the galaxies were on the move, most of them slipping rapidly away from each other and from us. The more distant the galaxy, the faster it was receding. Not only was the universe not static, *it was undergoing dynamic expansion.*

The implications of Hubble's remarkable discovery were not immediately apparent, even to Hubble himself. Some ideas are just too big to be processed quickly. It took two more decades and the concerted efforts of men like Georges Lemaître, George Gamow, and others to put the issue on the table: If the future was taking the galaxies farther and farther apart, then it stood to reason that in the past they must have been closer together. So close, ultimately, that matter's compression (due to the effects of gravity) might result in what Einstein's equations predicted to be a *singularity,* a point where the laws of the universe would simply break down.

The conditions immediately preceding this jaw-dropping event would have been hotter than any hell one can possibly imagine because that's what happens when matter is compressed. This fact of physics pointed to clues that eventually made the case for a cosmic explosion as the event that kicked off the expansion of the universe. Georges Lemaître, a Belgian priest conceived the idea, and British astronomer Fred Hoyle, in jest, coined the term "Big Bang" to describe the explosion.

"Bang?" you ask. "As in a very big noise?"

Well, no. A noise, big or little, requires a medium to carry the sound waves (you may remember the promotional tagline for the movie *Alien:* "In space, no one can hear you scream"). It's not even accurate to speak of the Big Bang as an explosion. Rest assured, however, that were it to take place in your living room, it would make a very big noise indeed, because we are talking about something infinitely dense suddenly undergoing incredibly rapid expansion.

It is important to note, however, that it was an explosion of space itself and not an explosion in any existing space. In the expanding universe today, it is space between galaxies that is expanding. As we shall see, there was no space before; it appeared along with the bang.

George Gamow theorized in the 1940s that the intense fireball of the Big Bang would leave an "afterglow" throughout the universe. His calculations suggested that the expansion of the universe would cool the radiation of the primeval ball of fire, leaving traces to be found today in the form of microwaves.

In 1965, Arno Penzias and Robert Wilson, two young radio astronomers, were frustrated in their attempt to get a clean signal from the big new horn antenna at Bell Labs in New Jersey because of a constant hissing that seemed to come from all corners of the universe at all times. A microwave telescope is simply a big "ear" attached to some very sophisticated analytical equipment, and a big enough ear can pick up things that otherwise might not be "heard," just as Hubble's big telescope allowed him to see things previously unseen.

Though neither realized it initially, Penzias and Wilson had picked up Gamow's predicted microwave relic of the Big Bang. They were listening to the energy of creation, and this energy is everywhere.

If you are near a television, turn it on (for the sake of science). If you have cable, switch the set to a channel other than the receiving channel (usually, channel 3 or 4), and if you use an antenna, switch to a channel with nothing on. Now, take a moment to contemplate the static that you see on your screen. Let your eyes go a little lazy, until the dots begin to dance. You are in part looking at a very ancient fingerprint, because a percentage of that static is the microwave remnant of the birth of the universe.

The discovery of cosmic background radiation marked the beginning of cosmology as a reputable scientific discipline, far from its speculative, metaphysical antecedents.

But there was more dramatic evidence yet. The Big Bang model of creation comes with such astounding heat that only the heartiest forms of "matter" could have arisen in its immediate aftermath. In the beginning, there was mostly energy with just a light dusting of matter. Fundamental particles of matter, beginning with the elusive quark, gradually congealed from energy as the universe cooled by expansion. Here we see the truth of Einstein's little equation; we see energy *becoming* matter.

By one second after the Big Bang, the temperature had fallen to ten billion degrees, and the universe was like a giant thermonuclear reactor gradually cooling by expansion. Our accurate knowledge of the rate of nuclear processes, clocked in decades of laboratory experiments, allows us to predict the ratio of atomic elements that would be produced in such a reactor. Some of these predictions agree with observational data to an astounding degree of accuracy of one part per billion. This was, so to speak, the clincher, and now even the pope is said to believe in the Big Bang.

Within the first three to four minutes, the light atomic elements — mainly hydrogen and helium — were produced. Indeed, the first important acts of material creation in this universe took place in the time it takes to phone in an order for a cheese and pepperoni pizza (assuming you aren't put on hold). The heavier atomic elements, up to iron, were subsequently forged in stellar furnaces. The rest of the elements were literally made of cosmic dust borne on the shockwaves of exploding stars called supernovae.

But what was it that "banged"? How did it become a universe?

There were also several other persistent questions about the initial conditions of the universe. In particular, how did the universe come to be so smooth on the large scale (as indicated by a high degree of uniformity of the microwave background radiation) and yet be so lumpy, that is, clumped into stars, galaxies, and clusters of galaxies, on the "local" scale? How had the universe reached such an advanced age without either collapsing in on itself by force of gravity or flying apart from the thrust of expansion? The rate of this expansion had to be very finely tuned indeed to have allowed the cosmos to survive to the present day. And, most puzzling of all, what had produced the enormous energy of the Big Bang itself?

Enter particle physicist Alan Guth, who in 1979 proposed *inflationary theory* as a means to answer these questions. This is not the sort of inflation that government finance ministers wrestle with, but a colossal physical inflation of the very early universe — an expansion almost unimaginably faster than the normal expansion observed today.

To determine where the cosmic fireball itself came from, we depend primarily upon the results of investigation of high energy particle physics for a picture of conditions at the beginning. The universe would have been much smaller and the temperature increasingly higher as we move toward the bang. Such temperatures are available only in particle accelerators today.

In turn, the particle physicists look to the relics of the events of the early universe to provide support for their theories.

At temperatures higher than what is attainable by super-colliders, the only resource available for particle physicists is the study of the early universe itself. This symbiotic relationship of particle physics (which deals with the smallest) and cosmology (the study of the largest) has provided essential forensic links in our investigation of the origin of the universe.

Also, thanks to the COBE (Cosmic Background Explorer) satellite, the Hubble space telescope, and a host of other eyes in the sky as well as the availability of high-speed computers, we can probe the cosmos as never before, using the entire spectrum of electromagnetic radiation from radio waves to gamma rays. This allows us to examine the universe in unprecedented detail and to continue uncovering cosmic relics like those that have ushered in what has been called the golden age of cosmology.

The Hubble space telescope has presented us with the first-ever image of a black hole, providing solid evidence that, indeed, the mass energy of tens of billions of galaxies can be packed into an insignificant niche, just as is thought to have been the case in the early universe. As you may have learned in school, when we gaze far out into space with the benefit of wondrous tools like the Hubble telescope, we are looking back in time, because it takes billions of years for the light to reach us from a galaxy far away. Through the looking glass of Hubble, which thus serves as a kind of time machine, these early galaxies, which evolved a few billion years after the Big Bang, look less elegantly symmetric than the more regular galaxies we observe closer at hand, thus providing another clue to the growth of the baby universe into adulthood. We are quite literally seeing these formative galaxies as they were before they attained the shape of maturity.

But in order to witness the birth pangs of the universe, we have to look much further back in time. The various stages of unification discussed in the previous chapter provide a basis for counting down to the moment of delivery. The unification of electromagnetism and the weak force must have existed when the temperature of the fireball was a thousand, trillion degrees and the cosmos only a ten billionth of a second old. Back to this point we are quite confident of our story because we can reproduce such conditions in the particle physics lab.

What happens when we back up further still, to even higher temperatures and greater density? The most breathtaking answer comes by way of the COBE satellite. With its ear trained on the murmur of the cosmic background radiation, COBE has detected minute variations in the primordial fabric of spacetime: stretch marks of the cosmic dawn. These scars appear like hieroglyphic squiggles, smeared across space by its inflationary expansion. (Remember; it is *space itself* that expanded with the Big Bang.) Stephen Hawking called these findings "the scientific discovery of the century, if not all time." *Newsweek* magazine dubbed them "the handwritings of God." Perhaps God, like many artists, likes to doodle a bit before committing himself!

What caused the stretch marks is stranger still. In an earlier chapter, we described how a vacuum quantum field is constantly fluctuating due to the uncertainty principle. And since Einstein showed that a field is a physical state of space itself, we can regard these fluctuations as wrinkles in spacetime. As space expanded nearly instantaneously due to inflation, these wrinkles were stretched out, thereby leaving scars.

These scars are detectable to us today by way of the exceedingly small variations in the temperature of microwave background radiation, and they are believed to be a consequence of the slight excess of matter accumulated in the spacetime wrinkles over a period of time following the expansion depicted by Alan Guth's inflationary model. To be fair, Guth had some help from Einstein, who long before had suggested that, under certain conditions, gravity could actually exert a negative force. That is, it could push rather than pull. Guth's pioneering work came from his study of the first blink of the awakened universe, when the GUT (grand unified theory) symmetry was intact and reality was far smaller than the head of a pin.

We are not equipped to envision how small a place it may have been. In truth the theorized size of the seed of the cosmic fireball can't even properly be called a place. It is, at most, one hundred millionth of a billionth the size of a single proton, which itself is about one thousand billionth the size of a grain of sand. And that is only if we grant the dignity of size at all.

Guth's breakthrough was to conjecture that when the GUT symmetry broke as a result of cooling due to the universe's expansion, there was what we might call a pregnant pause (technically, an instant of false vacuum, a vacuum of higher energy than normal), which caused a spike of negative gravity followed by an inflation of the cosmos by a factor of at least one followed by thirty zeros. Then, in less time than that number expressed as a fraction of a second, it was over, and the nuts and bolts business of universe making began, as inflation released a prodigious amount of energy in what is called a phase transition.

During inflation, space expanded much, much faster than even the speed of light; this super speed of expansion does not violate the speed limits imposed by Einstein's special theory of relativity (which posits that nothing can travel faster than light) because the theory is not applicable to the stretching of space itself. The enhanced spacetime wrinkles subsequently became the seeds for the formation of galaxies.

Let's take a moment to contemplate the wonders of creation. Although some of the details of the inflation process remain unclear, cosmologists generally agree on the fact that *something as enormously vast as our universe has emerged from an infinitesimally small nugget of space.* All the energy of the Big Bang fireball came, in effect, as a result of a moment of instability caused by the GUT symmetry breaking. The universe's essential traits were established as early as one hundred millionth of a billionth of a billionth of a billionth of a second from its inception. The inflation theory also implies that the cosmos is expanding in regions well beyond the edge of the visible universe (which itself has a hundred billion galaxies). That makes the cosmos inconceivably huge.

Because the universe was so tiny before that little pregnant pause, its content was in a state of thermal balance,
which explains why the temperature of the microwave
background radiation is so uniform and the raw material
of the young universe was more or less evenly distributed.

And as to why the universe does not collapse, inflation
adjusted the rate of cosmic expansion to a precision of better than one part in ten to the power of fifty or one followed
by fifty zeros. That's how finely balanced our universe
was when it started on the fulcrum between contraction
and eternal expansion, a Big Crunch or a Big Chill. One
smidgen of matter (energy) more or less and the universe
would have been either a shrinking violet or a runaway
train. That matter now includes you and me. So it is, in
fact, scientifically accurate to say that the universe would
not be complete without you.

The stretch marks in the microwave background radiation that the COBE satellite observed turned out to be the
cosmic Rosetta stone. In addition to giving a very accurate
age of the universe as 13.7 billion years, it has provided
strong evidence in support of the inflationary paradigm.
Although there are a few holdouts still waiting for a smok-
ing gun, most cosmologists now believe in the theory of
inflation.

Combined with other measurements, COBE data also
confirmed what the universe is made of today: 4.5 percent ordinary matter, 25 percent *dark matter* of an as yet
unknown composition, and about 70 percent of a mysterious factor known as *dark energy,* whose origin is as
elusive as any will-o'-the-wisp. Dark energy has an effect

of negative gravity similar to that which drove the cosmic inflation. Finding the source and nature of the dark energy is in many ways today's Holy Grail of cosmology, but could it simply be a rose by another name?

Inflationary theory also tells us something remarkable about energy. The process of inflation created all the *positive* energy in the universe, but at the same time it created an equal amount of *negative* energy, in the form of the mutual gravitational attraction of the stuff of the universe (every particle is drawn to every other particle in the cosmos). Mathematical analysis shows that the sum total of positive energy in the universe *equals* the sum total of negative energy. Therefore, strange as it may sound, the total energy of the universe is zero. Alan Guth famously remarked, "It is said that there's no such thing as a free lunch, but the universe is the ultimate free lunch."

So here's a Zen paradox to occupy your mind while performing some tedious task. The principle of conservation of mass-energy states that a system can never end up with more (or less) energy than the amount with which it started. But wait a second; how can something as big, bright, and busy as the universe have zero energy? A hint: It can, if the energy of inflation arose from something else, something with a value of zero.

We will address this conundrum further in a following chapter. For the moment we will proceed with our investigation on the now well-grounded presumption that the cosmic fireball of the Big Bang did, in fact, *arise from the process of inflation.* The universe's biography now accounts for everything in its nearly fourteen-billion-year history but for a very tiny fraction of a second after its moment of creation. The trail of evidence has led our detective to the edge of a cosmological Niagara Falls, where he stands, wondering whether he will ever find the body because the sudden rush of inflation has erased all the evidence.

Now what?

Until further evidence is found, the only thing our gumshoe can do is to turn metaphysical. In fact that's what has happened to physics. At least for now, physics has become almost indistinguishable from metaphysics. We don't know whether science will ever be able to cross this boundary, to say with certainty what came before "Once upon a time. . . . " So even tenured professors in Ivy League universities are speculating to their heart's content and can be proven neither wrong nor right. In the spirit of these Platonic times, I would like to present what seems reasonable to me.

Using Einstein's equations, Roger Penrose and Stephen Hawking have offered convincing theoretical analyses to show that classical spacetime ultimately collapses to a singularity (a point with zero dimension). But before reaching such a singularity, quantum effects should come to the rescue near Planck's dimension. If we were, then, to penetrate the veil of inflation and proceed toward Planck's dimension, what might we find?

We already have semiquantitative proof that near Planck's dimension, the strength of all the fields of nature becomes equal and they behave simply as different aspects of a single, *primary field*. Physicists and cosmologists generally agree that as we move back in time toward the origin of the universe, we would, at appropriate temperatures, witness the various stages of unification that the particle physicists envision.

So it would be reasonable to presume that the universe originated in a unity of all fields at or near Planck's dimension. At this stage, assuming the initial conditions for the birth of a universe can be determined, "the two fundamental laws of physics, for the elementary particles and the universe," as Nobel laureate Murray Gell-Mann has said, "become a single law."

Can science ever answer what was there before the beginning? When we talk about "before," we are talking in terms of time. Is it even reasonable to ask what happened in a time before time itself began, or are we stepping on God's toes? Stay tuned for some interesting ideas.

17

The Universe and Us

SUPPOSE THEY GAVE a party and nobody came.

Many of us have heard this expression, but it is probably safe to say that few of us have pondered its philosophical implications. Who are they? Is it a party if nobody comes? What kind of a party would it be if the people in attendance did not see the host? Let's frame the question another way: Suppose a universe was made and nobody was there to see it?

Scientists and philosophers tie themselves up in knots of abstraction over things that seem self-evident to most of us. However, behind such seemingly pointless debates lie some very profound enigmas. Pondering these riddles, scientists have lately warmed up to an idea they once considered unscientific.

The idea goes by the esoteric name of weak anthropic cosmological principle. The essence of the principle is that if the initial conditions and the natural constants of our universe were not exactly what they are, there would be no one here to observe it, much less to inquire into its origin. The principle's corollary is awe-inspiring; it suggests that the conditions were such at the moment of the creation of our universe as to presage eventual emergence of intelligent life in it.

The human mind's ability to understand the laws of nature has presented many eminent scientists with a mystery. Einstein expressed it cogently when he said, "The most incomprehensible fact about nature is that it is comprehensible." Distinguished British mathematician Roger Penrose is also bemused by the fact that the universe has developed in obedience to laws that our consciousness seems designed to grasp. Nobel laureate Eugene Wigner also referred to the double miracle of the existence of the laws of nature and the human mind's capacity to divine them. The anthropic principle provides a means for reconciling these two miracles.

Stephen Hawking, who is adorned today with Einstein's mantle of public esteem, cautiously allows in *The Universe in a Nutshell* that "few people would quarrel with the utility of some weak anthropic arguments." But then he asserts more strongly that "the anthropic principle can be given a precise formulation, and it seems to be essential when dealing with the origin of the universe." Examining the details of the universe, eminent physicist Freeman Dyson also finds that "the universe in some sense must have known that we were coming." This is about as close as a scientist will come to acknowledging that the party was given with the expectation that we would attend.

The anthropic principle seems to offer a unique solution for the particular way our universe came to be. At its inception, the entire universe was much smaller than an atom and, therefore, subject to the laws of quantum physics. This means that the universe could have begun in many possible ways. The anthropic principle *can* be factored in, thus requiring that the evolution of intelligent beings be a necessary condition for the beginning of the universe. In his book *At Home in the Universe,* John Wheeler, one of the most thoughtful scientists of our time, is even more emphatic. He concludes from his extensive studies of quantum mechanics that "It is incontrovertible that the observer is a participator in genesis." *The observer.* That's consciousness, and we are conscious agents, vehicles for manifestation of a potentiality that was there from the start.

A skeptic might argue: Isn't it absurd to think that this enormous visible universe with its hundred billion galaxies each containing a hundred billion stars and their countless planets would be needed to produce life on just one planet? The answer has less to do with the size of the universe, which inevitably results from expansion, than with the duration of time it takes to make the heavy elements necessary for life as we know it.

Remember from the previous chapter that the primeval stuff the early universe generated was mainly the light elements, hydrogen and helium. The heavier elements are produced by thermonuclear reactions in stellar furnaces, which takes billions of years. For the universe to exist this long, without falling in on itself, it *had* to expand to the incredible size we observe today. We can't help it if we happen to occupy just one small part of it.

And despite the word "anthropic," which refers to the creation of human beings, nothing about the anthropic principle requires that earthbound humans be the only ones turning a curious gaze back upon creation. There is compelling reason to believe that life is not unique to this earth. Some primitive life forms are thought to have been present on Mars at earlier times. The SETI program (Search for Extraterrestrial Intelligence) continues to scan the universe, and there is a scheme to detect signs of life beyond our solar system on NASA's drawing board.

Even if life is not found anywhere else, sober scientists, not merely *Star Trek* fans, believe humans themselves could populate most of the visible universe, given several billion years of time. If this sounds preposterous, consider the fact that in a few million years, a species of hominid that originated in a small sector of sub-Saharan Africa came to occupy every corner of our globe.

The scientific orthodoxy has not yet fully embraced the anthropic principle. Those willing to support the principle are careful to add quantum conditions, lest religious ideas be allowed to infiltrate pure science. For example, some propose that our universe is but one hamlet in a multiverse, a hamlet in which the natural laws just happen to be suitable for the emergence of life. The major problem with the multiverse concept is that there is no way to confirm the actuality of any other universe. Until we find at least a hint of the existence of another universe, the multiverse theory, alluring as it may be, will remain in the speculative domain.

We are probably best advised to deal with the universe we can genuinely observe, and press forward with the most provocative and exciting inquiry: What is the nature and effect of our observership?

John Wheeler strongly believes that "in defining any useful concept of reality" we have to take into account "the indispensable place of the participating observer — evidenced in quantum mechanics." The foregoing cannot really be true unless consciousness is as essential an aspect of nature as are the fields that give rise to force and matter and the primary field that gave rise to them. In fact, I can venture an opinion, supported by many whose names have appeared on these pages, saying: *consciousness itself is fundamental if not primary.*

But of what possible thread is consciousness spun? What is this subjective "I" (or, more precisely, this collective "we") that simultaneously projects itself into the vastness of the cosmos and reflects back upon its own nature?

In spite of much evidence to the contrary, many scientists dismiss consciousness as a mere by-product of the brain's electrochemical activity. They believe determinedly that a rational basis for consciousness can be found in the study of neural activity, but until recently, neuroscience itself gave little thought to the subject. We were told that we "saw" the moon's reflected light in the optical area of our brain and that any *awareness* of seeing it was either an emergent property of brain activity or an epiphenomenon (literally, brain chemistry causing our sense of experience).

Neuroscientists are now using functional magnetic resonance imaging (fMRI) machines to map the brain's response to various experiences, and they have had significant success identifying the neural correlates of such experience. But they haven't a clue as to how these neural correlates give rise to what you and I characterize as *experience*.

The only reliable detector of consciousness is another conscious being. As a result, consciousness, like spirituality, has always given rationalistic science a headache, and this has led to some strange conjectures.

In the early eighteenth century erudite English churchman and philosopher Bishop George Berkeley proposed that material reality had no independent existence outside the mind, consisting solely of God's projected thoughts. This radical idea might still elicit a knowing chuckle from the creators of the *Matrix* movies, but as far-fetched as it sounds, we must consider the context of Berkeley's extreme idealism, for less than a century earlier, mind had been severed from matter by the finely honed intellect of René Descartes, one of the most influential thinkers in humankind's history.

Before we turn to the question of how mind and matter might be reunited after nearly four centuries of estrangement, it may be wise to introduce a few of the terms and assumptions employed by neuroscientists and physicists involved in the bold new field of consciousness studies.

It seems clear that what we call "mind" is, in part, a process that enfolds a multitude of functions at ascending levels of complexity and refinement. The vast majority of these functions take place below the threshold of consciousness and account for what keeps us alive and ticking (the most basic is the regulation of our heartbeat). Furthermore, these functions are firmly rooted in the brain's oldest structures, structures we share with the animal world. This is demonstrated in the laboratory as we watch various sectors of the brain respond to stimuli, and the notion of a direct correspondence between brain function and behavior carries us quite a long way up the escalator, past the departments that deal with behavior that we describe as instinctual and sensory and well into the area of learning.

So far, the mind appears to be a bottom-up construction, an electrochemical computer programmed by the brain's evolution over millions of years. Many neuroscientists assert that the brain's computational skills offer a solution for the "easy problem" of consciousness: how we discriminate, categorize, and integrate information; focus our attention; and work out answers to life's basic survival questions.

Few in the scientific establishment take issue with eminent neuroscientist John Searles' assertion that "all the stimuli we receive from the world are converted by the nervous system into variable rates of neuron firings at the synapses." In other words, everything we perceive becomes an electrochemical signal, and the actual perception takes place in the brain, where the signals are decoded.

But even a bottom-up theorist like Searles draws the line with those proponents of artificial intelligence who contend that it's only a matter of time before a computer exists which can think as well as we can. "Nothing," he states, "is intrinsically computational." As we ascend to the next level of brain functions, something happens that cannot be explained easily by brain chemistry or algorithms. We become conscious agents. We no longer simply sense and behave, like automatons; we experience, and we affect experience.

First-person experiences, what scientists call *qualia,* constitute the "hard problem" of consciousness. With apologies to HAL, the sensitive cyborg in Stanley Kubrick's *2001: A Space Odyssey,* no computer exists that can form a thought construction like, "You won't believe what happened to me today!" because no computer exists that has an awareness of experience. In books like *The Emperor's New Mind* and *Shadows of the Mind,* Roger Penrose argues forcefully that no computer ever can, because "consciousness, in its particular manifestation in the human quality of understanding is doing something that mere computation cannot."

Penrose further insists that "a scientific world-view which does not profoundly come to terms with the problem of conscious minds can have no serious pretension of completeness. Consciousness is part of our universe, so any physical theory which makes no proper place for it falls fundamentally short of providing a genuine description of the world."

The more we think about it, the harder it becomes to deny that consciousness, the very window through which we eventually gather our prized scientific knowledge, is an integral part of the universal reality. Nobel physicist Eugene Wigner states it eloquently: "The principal argument is that thought process and consciousness are the primary concepts, that our knowledge of the external world is the content of our consciousness and that the consciousness, therefore, cannot be denied." By his famous pronouncement "Cogito, ergo sum" — I think, therefore I am — even Descartes, who is recognized for the Cartesian divide between mind and matter, premised his arguments based on the primary reality of consciousness.

The concept of consciousness as an epiphenomenon (a secondary phenomenon resulting from another phenomenon) was compatible with mechanistic classical physics, where the observer could be kept separate from the observed. The advent of quantum physics forever altered this picture. In quantum physical experiments, an observer's consciousness is *capable* of bringing about a particular outcome from the coexisting possibilities inherent in any quantum system. Thus, quantum physicists have achieved a victory of sorts in their debate with Einstein by demonstrating beyond any reasonable doubt that *observer and observed are fundamentally connected; their relationship is interactive and participatory.*

Although numerous experiments demonstrate this relationship, one of them reveals this most vividly. It is called the *entanglement* or the *nonlocality* experiment. It is known as EPR, after the thought experiment proposed by Einstein, Podolsky, and Rosen back in 1935, and its purpose was to disprove quantum mechanics. Being a visionary, Einstein realized that if the description of the world implicit in quantum mechanics were true, it would augur for a radically different view of reality.

The techniques and equipment required to perform EPR's thought experiment in the laboratory were not available until recently. Ironically, the very "impossibility" of an influence being faster than the speed-of-light that Einstein believed would be quantum physics' undoing turned out to be one of its signature proofs.

Focusing an intense laser beam on a special crystal, scientists created a pair of twin photons that shared their common properties, and then sent them off in opposite directions. Such photons are called *quantum physically entangled* since neither twin has a unique property of its own. Their properties simultaneously coexist in each of them! However, when we measure a particular property of one twin, the other twin instantaneously responds and displays the complementary property, and this remains true even if an arbitrarily large distance separates the twins. On the face of it, this defies the cosmic speed limit: the velocity of light. A variety of experiments have been performed along this line, always producing the same result.

These experiments not only demonstrate the participatory relationship between the observer and the observed; they have been utilized to achieve a form of *quantum teleportation* once thought to belong to the realm of science fiction. By superimposing some property of a third photon on one of the twins, the superimposed marker is also instantly teleported to the other twin, wherever it is. This has been done for entangled electrons as well, opening up the possibility that in some future epoch we could reconstruct a physical mass, particle by particle (assuming enough information can be teleported). Maybe one day we will truly be able to say, "Beam me up, Scotty!"

Ordinarily we think of space as that which separates objects. But the nonlocality experiments have demonstrated that if we send twin photons off to different sectors of space, any action performed upon one instantaneously affects the other, as if they remained forever bound in spite of their spatial separation. The implications of this nonlocality are truly jaw-dropping, for it implies that the most distant corner of the cosmos could be, in a quantum-entangled sense, as close as the tip of your nose. It's no wonder that Einstein referred to such phenomena as "spooky actions at a distance"!

In the quantum world, particles display bizarre behaviors that physicists, in desperation, call quantum weirdness. For example, a quantum particle can occupy more than one place or take more than one path at the same time. This simultaneous coexistence of all possibilities is known as coherent superposition or *quantum coherence.* (Coherence literally means "to stick together," or, more poetically, the harmonious relationship of all possibilities in a quantum system.) If all of this sounds creepy to you, as well, you're in good company. Nobel physicist Niels Bohr quipped, "If anybody says he can think about quantum physics without getting giddy, that only shows he has not understood the first thing about it." And fellow laureate Richard Feynman adds, "I hope you can accept Nature as she is — absurd."

Perhaps the most important feature demonstrated by the entanglement experiments is the existence of this counterintuitive coherent superposition, which, according to Erwin Schrödinger, is at the heart of quantum physics.

While such a scenario is hard to visualize, nevertheless it can be represented mathematically using the Schrödinger equation.

Before the stunning demonstration of entanglement, there was a general impression that scientists probably made up the coherent superposition of the quantum world to describe something they really did not know. Even the scope of the Schrödinger equation was thought to be questionable although it had been used for nearly three-quarters of a century to accurately predict results. This opinion changed dramatically when physicist John Bell came along and suggested some definitive experiments to verify particular predictions of the Schrödinger equation.

Bell's theorem and its conclusive experimental verifications have finally convinced the scientific community that the behavior of quantum particles, in terms of the Schrödinger equation, is precise. David Bohm and Basil Hiley isolated a part of the Schrödinger equation, which they call the quantum potential. This potential does not diminish with distance, which implies nonlocality. Hiley maintains that the quantum potential represents an *internal energy* with "features more akin to a self-organizing potential" indicative of nonseparability as well as participation.

The participatory aspect of the quantum potential allows the universe to function and evolve in the absence of an observer. Einstein, a fervent champion of common sense, famously squabbled with the quantum physicists over the matter of whether or not the moon was still there when we weren't looking at it! Because of the participatory feature of the quantum potential, the moon would be there even when nobody is observing it.

What all this has to do with human consciousness resides in the thesis — advanced in varying ways by scientists such as Roger Penrose and Karl Pribram — that the brain enfolds within its finest levels a quantum coherent state. This suggestion depends on the fact that different regions in the brain provide different aspects of perception — perceptions such as visual, color, motion, shape — yet our consciousness forms a single image combining all these different aspects. Penrose believes in "some kind of large-scale quantum coherence, acting broadly across considerable regions of the brain." It is a bold, but by no means a reckless concept. An indication of the existence of such quantum states becomes apparent when we take into account discrete changes or quantum leaps in the state of our consciousness. One particular example is familiar to all. Nobody remembers the very moment he or she falls asleep.

Is it this coherence of our brain that is responsible for our remarkable ability to interact with the universe and achieve the state we describe by the word *understanding?* If this proves to be the case, and I believe it will, then the most critical and uniquely human of our attributes is also, in more than a figurative way, entangled with the source of existence.

Although its systematic study has only just begun, consciousness — in the opinion of some eminent scientists today — is an absolutely fundamental part of this universe and cannot simply be computed away or dismissed as airy metaphysics. As we have seen, their conviction is based firmly on a careful examination of the quantum nature of primary reality.

Also, having to embrace the concurrent existence of complementary properties to explain the quantum world — such as the simultaneous existence of an electron particle as well as an electron's wave nature — paves the way for science to find an essential link between consciousness and the primary field. From this viewpoint, the fundamental realities of the primary field and consciousness are inseparable aspects of the same underlying process.

David Bohm has named this underlying process the *implicate order*. Basil Hiley suggests: "Mind and matter are but different projections from this deeper implicate order where such a division does not exist." He also emphasizes that "the implicate order is not some woolly metaphysical construction, it is a precise description of the underlying process," which is supported by credible mathematical analysis.

Since coherent superposition is an inherent characteristic of the quantum world, space and time are not expected to be merely ordinary numbers at some level. At the deepest level of space, even the infinitesimal Planck's dimensions can be deemed as merely an expectation. Bohm and Hiley call this pre-space, which gives rise to John Wheeler's proposed pre-geometry. There is expectancy in the air that quantum physics has to take such a picture seriously, possibly requiring a richer formulation of quantum mechanics itself. At the pre-space level, according to Bohm and Hiley, the universe is an undivided whole — everything is connected to everything else, and made coherent by the self-organizing property of the quantum potential.

In pre-space, the potentialities of consciousness and the primary field are united through mutual participation on a universal scale. Put another way, the essence of the implicate order is the *one source* that enfolds both the primary field (the common source of at least everything physical) and consciousness. Based upon this thesis, it would be logical to infer that *the one source of the world's great spiritual traditions is grounded in scientific reality.*

Walter Moore, biographer of quantum visionary Erwin Schrödinger, claims that Schrödinger was intuitively influenced by the ancient Indian school of spiritualism known as Vedanta when he formulated quantum mechanics. Perhaps the concept of the oneness in Vedanta also led to Schrödinger's decade-long search for the unified field theory. From the Upanishads, Schrödinger finds it to be "really so simple and so clear: *Tat twam asi, this is you.*"

Schrödinger believed in the Vedic concept that all conscious beings are aspects of the same universal entity. Expressed in terms of our scientific worldview today, consciousness would be manifest when the individual brain's quantum state is in resonance with the cosmic potentiality of consciousness. After Schrödinger, we may humbly assert that we are all equipped to be tuners of the universal source of consciousness.

18

Healing the Wound

WHEN WE THINK OF Descartes' famous assertion, "Cogito, ergo sum," we tend to hear it as the supreme expression of Enlightenment belief in the power of human reasoning, when in fact it was the upshot of his struggle with grave doubts about whether one could be sure of anything at all. His remedy for this uncertainty was to postulate that there could be no capacity for doubt unless there existed an "I" to do the doubting, and the consequence of his severing mind from matter was an exclusive focus on what was objectively real, that is, material.

Descartes and his followers employed scientific *objectivity* to banish centuries of dark and often malignant superstition, but there is a flip side to the Cartesian dualism between mind and matter. For if there is, as he said, "nothing in the content of mind that belongs to matter and nothing in the content of matter which belongs to mind," then how can we be reconciled with our own bodies, let alone with one another or with the universal source we have spoken of?

Descartes called matter *res extensa* (extended substance), which was defined by its physical location in

space. Mind, in contrast, was *res cogitans* (thinking substance) and it had no fixed location at all. Matter answered
to the immutable laws of nature while mind answered only
to reason, which answered to an unknowable God. If we
think about it for a moment, we see that this is still the
way we look at things: internal and external, subjective
and objective, observer and observed, mind and matter.
Our very nature is split.

The only advancement — if it can be called such — on
Descartes' theories has been to declare that mental things
occur mostly in the brain, which is not much beyond Descartes' conjecture that matter interfaced with mind in the
pineal gland! Post-Enlightenment science proceeded to
take God out of the equation altogether, leaving the mind
either imprisoned within the walls of the skull or adrift in
a void of abstraction. For more than three hundred years,
consciousness has been a refugee in the universe.

Yet René Descartes had perceived that mind, like the
Neo-Platonic *nous*, was of a different order, and in some
manner was linked to the transcendent and the transpersonal. In this sense, as in so many historical cases, it is
not so much Descartes himself who bears responsibility
for the resultant damage, but those who turned his insight
into a rigid either/or dogma.

Cartesian dualism was the artifact of an ancient strain
that recognized a distinction between what we can think
and what we can sense. As we have seen, the Vedic *rishis*
spoke of the mind stuff of Brahman as the ultimate reality,
Plato wrote in his dialogues about the ideal forms of which
our world is only a pale shadow, and Jesus heralded a

Kingdom that was not of this world. Indeed, great thinkers have long sensed that consciousness in some way transcended the physical, but none of them gave such primacy to matter nor declared such a radical split between "I" and "that" as did the rationalistic children of Cartesian thought.

By pronouncing matter to be of an entirely different substance from mind, Descartes, who sought to elevate God from gross matter, had unwittingly made God irrelevant to nature. From this point until the advent of quantum physics, only that which could be measured, predicted, and placed on a grid was deemed real. This is what psychologist Max Velmans calls "the dominance of the third person perspective." Something is real only if it's "outside" of us. Speaking plainly, this sounds like a prescription for a kind of global insanity, but believe it or not, until now it has been the foundation of most empirical science. It is important to remember that this foundation had not always been so firm.

Throughout much of ancient history and prehistory, man perceived himself as a part of nature, a nature that was fully animate and ensouled. Whether monotheistic or polytheistic, man felt his God/gods to be close at hand. The desert-wandering Hebrew prophet was conscious of God in the wind that rattled through dry vegetation and penetrated his very bones, and deemed God to be of a spiritual nature, while the pagan priest in tropical Asia or deeply wooded Central Europe felt himself surrounded, if not possessed, by demons that were every bit as real (and often as capricious) as himself.

Such panpsychism (literally, soul through all) was not limited to aboriginal or primitive cultures; it infused the classical civilizations of Greece and Rome, and it extended into the high Middle Ages thanks to Aristotle's continuing influence. Panpsychism was certainly present in my native land of India, and it remains so even today in the little village where I was born. The separation between self and other was, at most, a thin veil. This mystical thread was woven even into the fabric of medieval Christianity, which perceived nature's works as infused with symbolic potency. A profound shift began to occur shortly after the pivotal year of 1600, for as we have seen, when Cartesianism removed mind from matter, it also removed most traces of the genuinely sacred from the everyday world.

Since then we have tended to dismiss the ancient ways as superstition, swept away by the great mechanistic discoveries of Enlightenment science. But science alone can not be saddled with the shift to materialism. Science is observation, analysis, and prediction, and these are strongly influenced by the currents of human thought. What currents caused the break between spirituality and science, the deep cut that I called, in the beginning of this book, the wound that must be healed?

In the West, the effect of the Inquisition, which imposed its own heavy-handed version of political correctness on the thirteenth through sixteenth centuries, cannot be underestimated. Descartes in his early years was keenly aware that Giordano Bruno was put to the stake for tenaciously supporting the Copernican model of the planetary orbits and that the pope spared Galileo only when he recanted most of the new astronomy he had helped to pioneer. In some sense, Cartesian dualism may have been influenced by the belief that it was safer to let the church tend to spirit while science addressed itself to matters of matter. Descartes may have hedged his bets.

But there is more to the story than politics and religion. History and psychology reflect one another, and few epochs have witnessed as radical a transformation of man's self-image as the span between the medieval and the modern times. Along with the development of science, technology, and narrative literature came a rapid inflation of ego-awareness which effectively screened each person from the world. Identity was crystallized in the concept of "I am" rather than in the more ancient notion of "Thou art." How did this come to pass? Although I agree with scientists like Erwin Schrödinger, Max Planck, and Roger Penrose that the potentiality for consciousness is at least as old as our universe, this doesn't mean that man has always been conscious in the same way. I am leery of computer models for human cognition, but it seems safe to say that the software utilized by our brains gets updated from time to time.

When Descartes reflected upon matter, he experienced "something else" doing the reflecting, something not of the same nature as sea, soil, and skin. This is how our language works. When asked how we can be sure that the dog is outside, we don't reply, "Because it barks," instead answering, "Because *I* hear it barking." We answer by way of our mind and ego. We *know* that our limbs are attached to us because our mind affirms it (and in the case of phantom limbs, our mind continues to do so even when the physical appendage is missing).

To paraphrase neurologist Karl Pribram, the "objective 'I' " has become detached from the "subjective 'Me,' " the *this* is separate from the *that*. Once it is postulated that the observing "I" is not an active participant in what it observes, one of two things happens. Either the universe becomes a vast, deterministic machine, with consciousness, to quote physicist Henry Stapp, lying "impotently, and hence without responsibility, outside the chain of causal events," or we must conclude, with Bishop Berkeley, that the physical world is nothing but a projection of the mind.

The first position is known as materialism and the second as idealism. While most people remain stubbornly mired on one side or the other, the discoveries of quantum physics have shown that neither position is correct. "I" and the universe somehow participate with one another. Mind affects matter and matter affects mind. Could the answer to the "why" of consciousness lie in John Wheeler's time-bending notion that our "observership brings the universe into being"?

It is arguable that after mind and matter had been put asunder consciousness needed time to integrate the new paradigms of individuality that took root in the Renaissance. The mind's software was updated, but now it is again obsolete.

The dilemma we face is that our science is racing far ahead of our sensibilities. We know that science has revealed a new order, but we cannot yet see it. As a result, most of us spend a good deal of time feeling vaguely out of phase, a condition that manifests itself as dis-ease. We sense that our brains are capable of laser-like clarity, but we cannot seem to access it.

If the great American psychologist William James was on the money when he stated, over a century ago, that "there is only one primal 'stuff' of which everything is composed," then it becomes possible to concur with David Bohm and Basil Hiley, who said that at some level of reality (in the pre-space/implicate order), mind and matter merge. At this sublime level, Descartes' *res extensa* and *res cogitans* are indistinguishable.

Bohm maintained that implicit in the quantum potential, as discussed in the previous chapter, was a "mind-like quality in matter," which he identified with the notion of *active information.* Even an electron, he argues, has a rudimentary "mental" aspect. If this is true, it's reasonable to ask whether our brains, as material outgrowths of this process, have evolved to operate in perfect resonance with this active information. "One could say," Bohm and Hiley allow, "that through the human being, the universe is making a mirror to observe itself."

Consciousness is clearly integrated with things like memory, attention, and, perhaps most closely, with language, all of which are presumed to have their locus in the brain itself. But consciousness is not simply in our heads. It's everywhere we are, and it's everywhere we are not. As we move in spacetime, we move through the potentiality of consciousness.

Some of the most fascinating and provocative ideas about consciousness come from the minds of two adventurous theorists: neurologist Karl Pribram and biologist Rupert Sheldrake. Pribram has developed a *holonomic model* in which memories are distributed over the entirety of the brain (as with an image on a holographic plate) rather than in localized traces. Pribram believes that the mind-brain relationship is top-down and that individual experience "partakes of a larger consciousness."

He also states (in "Consciousness Reassessed," 2004) that "just as gravity relates material bodies, consciousness relates sentient bodies." Like Roger Penrose, Pribram sees consciousness as more than mere chemistry or computing. It is, in his words, "associated with nonlocal activity among dendritic micro-processes rather than biochemical events associated with neural firing." If that sounds like Greek, don't be intimidated. It simply means that consciousness, like events in the quantum world, isn't something you can point a stick at.

Sheldrake has advanced the notion of an "extended mind" that can "reach out" to influence things well beyond the brain's boundaries. Like Nobel physicist Brian Josephson, he is deeply interested in finding a scientific explanation of psi phenomena such as telepathy. A convincing proof of such phenomena will obviously demonstrate that consciousness is not merely confined within the skull; it is capable of biological nonlocality.

However skeptical mainstream science may be of such theories, we are clearly moving toward some startling new

conceptions, and all seem to suggest that Descartes' depiction of mind as "something else" was not so much
wrong as wrongly understood. Our brain's ability to actual-
ize the potentiality of universal consciousness may make
us, in a sense, the eyes and ears of God. In the words of the
great German mystic Meister Eckhart: "The eye in which
I see God is the same eye in which God sees me."

The extent to which consciousness is top-down (that
is, it directs higher brain function) rather than bottom-up
(the result of brain function) may be debated for years
to come. But in the new paradigm of participatory consciousness suggested by the work of people like Wheeler,
Bohm, Hiley, and Pribram, there is no more talk of mind
being disengaged from the universe. Mind is entangled
with matter as matter is entangled with mind. *If René Descartes could not locate mind within matter, it may have
been because his road map of reality lacked the detail to
reveal the tiny districts of inner space.*

What significance does the new consciousness paradigm have for you and me in our daily lives? In a nutshell,
if the potentiality for consciousness is found to exist at the
very foundation of reality — if it is, in a word, basic — then
it stands to reason that to be fully conscious is to partake of
that potentiality as fully as our human design allows. Ordinary survival and comfort functions — such as heartbeat,
hunger, sex drive, and defense — will continue whether
we partake of greater consciousness or not. However, it
seems unlikely that humankind will either achieve its highest potential or reintegrate a genuine spirituality unless we
are able to tune ourselves to the transpersonal source.

By severing mind from matter, the Cartesian divide provided a justification for our thinking that we are not responsible for our actions, that our consciousness is merely a passive spectator to events. Contrary to the tenets of Cartesianism, the goal of this chapter — and perhaps of this book — has been to suggest a convergence between the most fundamental levels of physical reality and consciousness. Science now shows us that our consciousness plays an active role in determining our actions and bringing out specific manifestations of nature. We have also learned that we are a part of something much larger, which we have referred to as *one source*. Perhaps our sense of morality stems from the realization that we are indeed part of something much larger than ourselves. Therefore, our actions should be appropriate to what is implicit in that knowledge. When we act from this realization, we bridge the Cartesian divide of mind from matter and the wound it caused is healed.

19

When Science Meets Religion

THE AWARD-WINNING PLAY *Inherit the Wind* dramatizes one of the first great skirmishes in the ongoing conflict between evolutionists and creationists. A small-town schoolteacher by the name of Scopes was arrested for teaching Darwin's theory, and his subsequent trial pitted the brilliant (and agnostic) defense attorney Clarence Darrow against the passionately devout statesman and three-time presidential candidate William Jennings Bryan, in what became known worldwide as the Scopes Monkey Trial. (The play and subsequent film versions give all the characters pseudonyms.)

In perhaps the play's most memorable scene, Darrow (called Drummond and played in the film version by Spencer Tracy) puts Bryan (renamed Brady and played by Frederic March) on the stand and grills him about his religious objections to the theory of evolution. At the climactic moment, Darrow zeroes in on the seven days of creation from the book of Genesis and asks Bryan: "Now, couldn't that 'first day' actually have been, say, a year — or ten years — or ten million years?" "No!" storms an apoplectic Bryan. "The Bible says it was done in one day!"

"But God," counters Darrow, "can make a 'day' as long as he wants, can't he?" Red-faced, Bryan insists, "The Bible says he did it in one day!"

Leaning in close, Darrow delivers his coup de grâce: "Are you saying that the Bible's authority is greater than God's?" At this point in the play Bryan drops dead of a stroke, perhaps reflecting the playwright's judgment in the matter, but a point is made.

The present consensus among cosmologists is that the age of our universe is in the neighborhood of fourteen billion years. Such lengths of time cannot be processed by the human mind any more than the other extravagant numbers we've been tossing around, but scientists, mystics, and serious religious scholars of all persuasions have long suspected that the universe was very, very old, notwithstanding Biblical experts who purport to date its genesis to between six thousand to ten thousand years ago!

Humankind has always tended to deal with such great spans by condensing and grouping them into "ages," "epochs," "eons," or, in the Vedic system, *yugas*. For those readers who may have been taught according to the stricter timelines of some Judaic or Christian traditions, I would like to make something of a peace offering from the world of science.

Fourteen billion years are incalculable to us, but they may be only the length of an office worker's holiday to God. If science can assign nature its own units of measurement in Planck's dimensions, can't religion be entitled to assign God a time unit for creation, be it seven days or eternity? After all, science has no established idea about what happened before time began.

There really needn't be any great and gruesome conflict between religious cosmology and scientific cosmology. Reconciling them is mostly a matter of adopting a more analogical, less literal turn of mind. Schoolchildren, for example, might come to a clearer understanding of cosmological processes by way of myth and fable, whether the universe is represented as a tortoiseshell or a swirling maelstrom from which the hand of God commands the starry firmament. But St. Paul notes that when he became a man he "put away childish things." If I may extend the thought, we adults are to embrace the no less wondrous reality revealed to us by the chief instrument of science: the human mind.

Cosmology points to a likely scenario: A single field emerged at the origin of the universe, already containing within itself the blueprint of the physical universe, just as a human genome contains the plan for an entire human. Although we refer to this phenomenon as a field, it may be more appropriate to call it, simply, unification, since it cannot yet be identified with separate forces or particles. Therein lies yet another enigma, however, as we generally think of union as an end rather than a beginning, and this was quite evidently a unification endowed with a bright future. Is it too bold to think that the primordial single field, in some sense not yet clearly understood, triggered the onset of the universe, that it was, so to speak, the force that sailed a quadrillion stars?

Although it stretches the mind, we may visualize the seed of the universe as a "something with nothing around it," and one might imagine that such a seed — a *something* enfolding the potential for a whole universe — would long to sprout. Think, for example, of an ember. Can we not say, at least poetically, that it longs to be a fire? It requires only inspiration (from the Latin *inspirare,* which means to breathe into, as the God of Genesis breathed life into Adam). Or perhaps it requires a momentary instability, a cosmic tickle, the kind that triggers a sneeze. Scientists do talk about these things, though they are more likely to use arcane phrases like *quantum fluctuation, scalar field of symmetry breaking* or *false vacuum.* In any event, something cracked the cosmic egg, and, before that, something happened to upset the so-called pre-space of pure potentiality. Indeed, such a state leads to Wheeler's question: Did consciousness give rise to creation? And if not consciousness, what?

Whatever the case may be, the single field then unfolded to direct the construction of the universe in the sequence to which our evidence points. It gave rise to all the known fields and their material manifestations, in a ceaseless blossoming that might be likened to those gorgeous fireworks that keep on surpassing themselves long after we're sure they've given their best.

And once the single field had relinquished its primacy to gravity, electromagnetism, the nuclear forces, et al., did it cease to be? We can answer by way of analogy: Does the human genome cease to be once the human being is made? Decidedly not. As your local police department's forensics team knows, it's there even in the tiniest flake of skin. If we look closely enough at the fabric of space, we still ought to find indication of unification, albeit in an unmanifest way. To accomplish this, we need the help of quantum physics, as we discussed earlier, to guide us to Planck's tiny dimensions and the restoration of nature's symmetries.

The unimaginably high temperatures that prevailed at the beginning of time and welded the symmetries of the primary field no longer exist, not even in the center of the hottest stars. So how can unification still pervade space-time at its deepest level? Here quantum field theory points us to a startling bit of cosmic forensics: Nature at Planck's dimensions is equivalent to nature at the extremely high temperatures of the pre-inflationary period. Thus, the original single field abides, and the source is still with us. The source did not leave us, just as the God of religion did not abandon the world after creating it.

When we think of space, we tend to think of it as "out there," where the sky looks as black as coal and as empty as a poor man's cupboard. It's important to keep in mind, however, that this empty blackness resides in us, as well, for we are made of atoms, and inside an atom is mostly space. If we were to expand an atom to the size of a football stadium, its nucleus would be a tiny fly on the fifty-yard line, its electron cloud a dusty haze surrounding the cheap seats. The source is not only with us, it is within us.

Further, we now know that empty space is not empty at all. As we have seen, quantum field theory postulates that even the darkest sectors of the universe are occupied by a quantum vacuum that seethes with quantum frenzy. In recent years, proponents of the various string theories have asked us to squint still harder and accept the possibility that spacetime at Planck's dimensions is woven throughout with vibrating loops of "string," a bit like the multicolored loops we see when we turn over a Persian rug. Further, they suggest that the greater portion of these strings is compacted into as many as six or seven hidden dimensions beyond the four that make up spacetime.

As a violin string's rate of vibration determines its pitch, a superstring's mode of vibration determines what kind of particle it displays. This is an entirely new way of understanding how subatomic particles come to be, and it lends an almost tactile quality to the phrase "fabric of space." Of course, nothing on this infinitesimal scale is tactile, and string theory, at this juncture, remains a set of elegant mathematical abstractions in pursuit of experimental proof. Still, the notion of a universe of harmonious vibrations is sublime, and it meshes with some very ancient spiritual concepts. Could the deceptively plain fabric through which the loops are drawn be the fertile ground of the primary field?

Have we found the address for the Architect of the Universe? Some scientists, particularly those of John Wheeler's theoretical lineage, might offer a qualified "Yes." The more mathematically inclined quantum physicists may shake their heads "No" and continue to seek a finer and finer grain in the universe. One has to wonder, however, at what point we are, in the words of Zen philosopher Alan Watts, "trying to taste our own tongues." The fact is that neither side in the argument conclusively provides the first of the three fundamental types of evidence our cosmic detective needs to close his case. We have established *opportunity*. We have identified the *means*. But we are missing the *motive*.

To be fair, science has waltzed with the "why" question in the form of a multiverse and exotic mathematical constructs, but almost all such conjectures hand causation over to the same probabilities that drive a game of roulette. After all, we exist. Somehow, most likely by sheer serendipity, things clumped together in our favor.

Thus, to the question, "What came before the beginning?" orthodox science still whispers, "Nothing," and unwittingly passes the baton to the theologians as surely as René Descartes did in his day.

For those who are uncomfortable with the notion of something coming from nothing, the world's great spiritual traditions offer a timeless answer: God came before. Alone among all things, God is "uncreated." Most theologians and quite a few scientists are fairly content to leave it at that, for the beginning of time is a threshold none of us is likely to cross any time soon.

That leaves us with the ultimate unsolved mystery, stashed away in the police files of the first precinct on the ragged edge of space. At this, the doggedly curious TV detective Columbo might well have rubbed his chin and mumbled, "There's just one thing I'm not clear on. . . . "

We create an almost Aristotelian problem with a dichotomy by saying, "Science is science and religion is religion, and never the twain shall meet." If we give creation to God and all the rest to science, what need is there now of God?

The heart might answer that God — as expressed through love, devotion, morality, and ethics — provides for the well-being of souls while science takes care of the machinery. We could leave it at that: a bifurcated universe similar to Descartes', in which what used to be called "gross matter" falls under the laws of physics and the subtler stuff of spirit belongs to God. But that is a universe that relegates the beauty of a child or a blooming rose to the domain of widgets. This is a book that set out to find, in some small measure, common ground between fact and faith, so grit our teeth as we may, we cannot simply pass the buck. If we are to give more than lip service to the notion that God resides within us, then the buck stops here.

We must at least ask the question: What could the world of science tell us about the nature of God?

Recall that in our discussion of world religions, we made a distinction between the Western "nothing" and the Eastern concept of "nothing*ness*." Recall also that when we discovered that the universe today has a net energy of zero, we realized that it must have also started from a value of zero. We qualified this strange fact with the observation that — in the case of the cosmos — zero obviously amounts to more than nothing. As bizarre as it may sound, all of creation seems to have started from a mystical number which normally conjures an image of void to us. What could that mean?

As the notable science writer Charles Seife records in his book *Zero: The Biography of a Dangerous Idea*, zero has been an enigma to theologians, philosophers and mathematicians alike over the millennia. The mysterious number zero originated in India. In the seventh century, men such as Brahmagupta saw zero not merely as a place-holder but as an inviolable center between positive and negative numbers. Later in the twelfth century, the Arabic mathematician al Samawal wrote, "If we subtract a positive number from zero, the same number is produced as a negative value. When a negative number is subtracted from zero, it appears in its positive aspect."

Mathematicians have long recognized that zero is invariably connected to infinity. When we divide something by infinity, we get zero; when anything is divided by zero, we get infinity. Zero appears as a vanishing point between positive and negative infinities. In other words, once we include negative numbers, could zero as easily stand for the source of everything as the realm of nothing?

It was not until well into the Middle Ages that Europe began to hail zero as representing the creative potential of God (creation ex nihilo) rather than as a symbol of that ultimate nihilist, the devil. By the 1600s, zero finally obtained worldwide legitimacy at the crux of all higher mathematics. We have seen that the late visionary physicist David Bohm did not stop at zero. He conceived of something transcending zero and named it the implicate order, which consists of the concurrent existence of all potentialities in the multidimensional pre-space. As we have discussed earlier, he suggests material reality and consciousness are projections from this implicate order.

Finally, there is Bohm's assertion that the implicate order enfolds the entire universe holographically, in that every part of itself echoes much of what we have said of the cosmic genome; like the human genome, every stitch of the universe contains the blueprint of the whole enchi-lada. It should be evident by now that you and I are part and parcel of this implicate order.

What are we really talking about here? What "immortal hand or eye," to quote Blake, could fashion such a mar-velous symmetry, one in which we can truly "see a world in a grain of sand"? Since it is sensible to believe that some-thing like Bohm's implicate order does exist and is the agent of the universal potentiality of consciousness, then we may at last have found a ship that will sail us beyond the Big Bang, a story that will tell us what happened before "Once upon a time." Though it may not close our detec-tive's case with a verdict that is beyond all reasonable doubt, we may, perhaps, have seen a faint glimmering of the nature of God and of how the abundant majesty of the cosmos arises from an address numbered zero.

Transcending all theologies and denominations, human-kind has had a conviction of a creator divinity, which, hav-ing brought the universe into existence, remains present throughout it, upholding the ongoing creation. People seem to have always accepted that the Creator will never be revealed to us empirically. Yet for eons we have deemed this divinity worthy of adoration and have directed ardent prayers to it, making it the vessel of our hope. Now, I believe for the first time in human history, we find remarkable support from science for the *one source* of religion. We have objective knowledge of an abstract entity that permeates the entire universe. Inseparable association of that universal entity with consciousness also appears credible.

In the previous chapters we have seen that there are solid scientific reasons supporting the basic insight of quantum field theory — namely that the primary elements of reality are the underlying fields, which we've learned fill all space and time. Physicists are close to proving that all these fields arise from a primary field. If true, it could be argued that this primary field, having spawned the universe, is now present at the very fabric of space throughout the universe. Would this field therefore be orchestrating the very foundational aspects of at least everything physical? Remember also Bohm's logical notion of the implicate order, which can enfold the primary field and consciousness. Think of the cosmic potentiality of consciousness in pre-space, where all potentialities are presumed to be in quantum coherence, and it is reasonable to assume the feasibility of just one source, as envisioned by the world's various spiritual traditions.

We have to keep in mind that science is always a work in progress. Centuries or even decades from now, new vistas are sure to open up in the scientific landscape. It may then provide a better answer to the "why" question. For now, it is amazing that science is meeting the core of religion and that the two are stimulating each other, as Einstein believed they always would.

20

Return to Coherence

WE ARE OBSERVING an experimental test subject. Not a laboratory rat nor a monkey, but a man practiced in the ancient art of meditation. He sits in half-lotus position atop a massage table, a dozen or more silver chloride electrodes affixed to his scalp, strain gauges girdling his abdomen and thorax, and devices attached to his right thumb and forearm monitoring his pulse and blood pressure. He is calm but supremely attentive as the experimenter directs him to commence meditation.

After only a few minutes, remarkable things begin to happen. The subject's rate of respiration decreases from an already quite relaxed eleven breaths per minute to only five breaths per minute. His blood pressure drops, and his skin's electrical resistance increases. The EEG recording his brainwave activity displays a marked synchrony across all regions of his brain, with a predominance of alpha waves, the rhythms most associated with profound relaxation. Yet, he is not asleep. Quite the opposite. He is keenly aware of everything his mind is doing.

In the preceding chapter we explored what it means to be conscious and the astounding notion, supported by quantum physics, that the universe may be, in some sense, aware of itself. Further, we saw that this universal form of awareness — a quantum potentiality of conscious- ness implicit everywhere in the cosmos — might somehow be linked with the source of creation. If we, as John Wheeler, David Bohm, and others have argued, are par- ticipants in this creation, then it's reasonable to ask: What would it be like to share, for even a few minutes a day, in the universe's awareness of itself?

An answer may be found in one of the oldest forms of "exercise" known to humankind: the practice of medita- tion.

In most of Asia (and, increasingly, in the West as well), meditation has been inseparable from religion, for religion is not principally a matter of tenets but essentially is a mat- ter of experience. The core experience, as we have seen, is described almost identically by mystics of all faiths as an altered sense of space and time, the dissolution of self and ego, and a perception of being somehow unified with the *one source* of all. The poet laureate Rabindranath Tagore of India, who was also an accomplished mystic, expressed it through a poem in my native Bengali:

Being immersed in the ocean of nectar, I transcend
the manifest creation, the sun and the moon appear
     melded,
and I discern no space, no time, nor any boundary.
Only the image of love springs forth in my heart.
The ecstasy seems uncontainable.

Although some elegance of his expression might have been lost through my translation, I believe it essentially represents the feeling that occurs during deep meditation. With the insight gained from our review of modern science, we may see how closely this nonlocal sense of being corresponds with the world depicted by quantum physics.

The physical universe revealed to us in the last century by men such as Albert Einstein, Edwin Hubble, Niels Bohr, Erwin Schrödinger, Richard Feynman, and Alan Guth may appear to us at first as disturbingly chaotic and violent. Phenomena such as black holes and particles that flit in and out of existence cause us to question the stability of the world around us. Indeed, a measure of existential uncertainty may be the price of intellectual maturity, for it is a maturity that brings with it a high degree of anxiety. We sometimes doubt the solidness of the ground beneath our feet.

Likewise, modern psychology has revealed a roiling, primitive subconscious beneath the orderliness of our rational minds, a dark place full of selfish and often violent impulses. We question our fellow man's goodwill, and we are inclined to see a Mr. Hyde within every Dr. Jekyll, a beast lurking in the shadow of every beauty. Heaven seems more distant than ever.

But there is compelling evidence, in the sciences of both matter and mind, of an abiding calm behind the storm, a coherence beneath the chaos. This calm resides in what David Bohm called the implicate order. At this deepest unmanifest level, we can presume there is a coherence as steady and strong as in the pulse of a laser. This is the state we navigate toward by means of what I will refer to as quantum meditation, for if we are able to access the coherence behind the static of our stress-ridden daily lives, our own light will shine more brightly.

Why "quantum meditation"? Is this simply a twenty-first-century repackaging of something as old as the hills? In part, the answer is yes. The fundamental process of meditation does not vary, whether it is labeled Transcendental Meditation, qigong, mindfulness, or tai chi. Dr. Herbert Benson clearly elucidated these techniques for Western readers in 1975 in *The Relaxation Response.* This little book became a big best seller and legitimized for many Americans the practices embraced a decade earlier by the Beatles under the tutelage of their guru, the Maharishi Mahesh Yogi, founder of Transcendental Meditation.

Benson, a cardiologist and researcher at Harvard Medical School, discovered a connection between stress and high blood pressure. Everyday conflicts tend to trigger our instinctive fight-or-flight response, signaling the brain to release massive quantities of hormones like adrenaline and increase blood flow to the muscles. This hardwired reflex, a function of the autonomic nervous system and some of the oldest parts of the brain, is very useful when facing a charging lion, but considerably less so when facing an angry boss. In most of the stress-producing situations we face today, it is not appropriate to either fight or take flight, so we stew in our own juices, damaging our mental and physical health. Is it then any surprise that stress has become such a killer in our society?

Dr. Benson and other pioneers, like Robert Keith Wallace, formerly of the Center for the Health Sciences in Los Angeles, and those who followed their lead subsequently found that practitioners of Transcendental Meditation and other age-old forms of meditation were able to override their autonomic nervous system by exercising their brain's higher functionalities, specifically those connected with the left prefrontal lobe, the zone most closely associated with attention, creativity, and conceptualization. As marvelous as it seems, evolution has equipped us with the tools to heal the damage done by stress.

But that is only the half of it.

The physical effects of meditation include reducing the heart rate, blood pressure, and oxygen consumption; lowering production of stress hormones and blood lactates; and bolstering the immune system. These are the fringe benefits in this meditation compensation package. The real earnings are in the effect upon consciousness itself: during meditation a quantum leap into a different state with an associated feeling of immense bliss, and afterwards the ability to act with a great clarity of mind and an innate sense of fulfillment.

Let us examine statements on the effects of meditation by two experts on the mind and brain. The first statement is a clinical description from a paper by Alarik Arenander, Ph.D.:

"The coherent integration of cortical-thalamic processing loops [in meditation] would lead to a global state of neural integration. . . ."

Translation: The brain's ancient, instinctual parts are brought into phase with the brain's higher functions, resulting in a state of profound lucidity. The ground rises up to meet us; the beast is tamed.

The second statement is a description from Roger Thompson, Ph.D., a psychologist in private practice in Chicago:

"[In meditation] we recognize that the true nature of individuals is emphatically non-individual.... "

This brief assertion is remarkable in that it can be applied equally well to the most ancient insights of the mystics and the most up-to-the-moment revelations of quantum physics.

Recall what we have seen about the layers of material reality: that as we submerge ourselves in the sea of subatomic particles, descending through the ceaseless flux of energy, what we find when we "touch bottom" is an undivided whole, a potentiality in which each and every part is somehow aware of, and affected by, the others.

Now consider quantum physics, with its experimental proofs of things like nonlocality and entanglement, of which the physicist Michio Kaku wrote, "of all the theories proposed in this [the twentieth] century, the silliest is quantum theory.... The only thing quantum theory has going for it is that it is unquestionably correct." This sentiment was prefigured when Einstein quipped, "The more success the quantum theory has, the sillier it looks." A brief review of the famous double-slit experiment — which Richard Feynman called both "the heart of quantum mechanics" and its most enduring mystery — further illustrates the confounding nature of quantum physics.

In modern applications of the double-slit experiment, single photons of light or subatomic particles such as electrons are fired one at a time at a screen in which two narrow slits have been cut. On the far side of the screen is a photographic plate or a detector that registers the hit. What we now know, of course, is that the detector shows not only a point of impact but an interference pattern characteristic of waves. The tiny quantum pilgrim has solved its dilemma by acting as both particle and wave, going through both slits at once! Faced with the choice of one possibility or the other, it has opted to allow for both. Only when we, as observers, limit the possibilities by closing a slit does the little shape-shifter "decide" that it is a particle after all!

Right now, as you read this, the same kind of either/or decisions are being made within the gray matter of your brain. And the observer — the hand that closes one of the slits — is consciousness. Think about it. For this to be true, consciousness must be something basic and complementary to the material stuff of our brains. Henry Stapp remarks that our free will, an inherent characteristic of consciousness, cannot be explained by any known physical law, strongly supporting the idea that consciousness is something fundamental.

Might the same consciousness allow us to escape our individual separateness and become blissfully entangled with the source of our existence? If we can free ourselves (and there is ample evidence that we can), then the first thing we might want to do is give our consciousness some room to work. Step back from the maelstrom, into a quiet space, relax, and let your mind wander away from stress.

Quantum meditation is a version of the timeless art, stemming from the realization that until our mind responds with choice, all possibilities remain open. We are, at this moment, unfolding from the implicate order.

This is spirituality infused by science. No less a personage than the Dalai Lama has said, "We should always adopt a [spiritual] view that accords with the facts [of science]." In this case, the two are completely in accord.

The simple techniques I will describe below are derived from the ancient Zen practice of *Vipassana* (insight), now called mindfulness meditation and recently profiled in *Newsweek* as a tool for making the "Mind-Body Connection." The concept of mindfulness received a compelling update in the work of the twentieth-century Buddhist scholar Nyanaponika Thera, who described it as bare attention, "a clear and pointed awareness of what actually happens to us and in us at each successive moment of perception." Although mindfulness is just one of many effective ways to get in tune with the self and with the *one source,* the meditator's observer role in the mindfulness technique makes it notably compatible with modern physics — we are both observing events and interacting with them. In a real sense, mindfulness makes us subject as well as object.

The setting for any type of meditation need not be an ashram or a Zen retreat in the mountains, though such places can be wondrously conducive to reflection.

A parked car in a quiet place at the side of the road will do, or any room in the house or apartment can serve as a sanctuary. Even a straight-backed chair in your office or cubicle can work, so long as you can obtain fifteen or twenty minutes without disruption. Overall, the actual setting is less important than the mindset, which is a factor of both your physical and emotional condition as well as your predisposition to the act of meditation.

In spite of abundant scientific evidence revealing the power of our minds over our bodies, most people still seem to ignore it. A careful look at the evidence should persuade you that consciousness can heal, and your efforts will bring a higher degree of coherence in your consciousness. Once you get a taste of the experience, you will know for sure that an innocuous process like meditation can bring a profound change in the quality of your life.

Let me continue briefly on some other aspects of mindset before proceeding to practice. The ability to let something happen, which is the essence of true relaxation, is different from the ability to sleep. Although falling asleep, like meditating, involves a quantum leap in consciousness, there are tense people who can nonetheless fall asleep almost as soon as their head hits the pillow. They simply turn off. This is not what we're after with meditation (if you fall asleep during *zazen* in a Tibetan monastery, you are liable to receive a whack on the shoulders from the master's *keisaku,* or "warning stick"). What we're after is relaxed attention, and the key word is attention. As any schoolchild knows, it is easier to pay attention when we are well-rested and healthy.

It is not my purpose here to dispense advice on diet, exercise, or emotional health, but it stands to reason that meditation will be most effective when our bodies and minds are in sync and in reasonably good shape. The practice of yoga, now quite popular in the West, was developed as a means of preparation for meditation. Even if you never master the lotus position, learning a few basic yoga stretches will aid in focusing and in gearing down for extended periods of stillness. If there is a cat in your home or neighborhood, watch how it periodically extends its front paws, drops its belly, and opens up (stretches) its spine. The well-known Child's Pose in yoga is based on this maneuver. But any moderate exercise, such as walking or swimming, will encourage a meditative mindset. For one thing, exercise triggers the release of brain chemicals known as endorphins, which are our body's natural opiates. Why reach for Vicodin when these are at hand?

Similarly, a diet anchored in whole grains and fruit will do more than any over-the-counter antacid to temper indigestion and engender a feeling of well-being. It is hard to hear our minds, let alone the hum of the cosmos, when our stomachs are rumbling. Gandhi managed quite well — across thousands of miles and through numerous hunger strikes — on raisins, nuts, and goat's milk. But we needn't go to that extreme. Just keep it light.

Finally, much experience indicates that dawn and dusk are the best times for meditation. But set, and keep, a time that suits your own schedule.

The mindfulness technique does not require a mantra or focusing device as is used in Transcendental Meditation and other forms of contemplative meditation. But only sitting in silence and trying to hear an inner voice is not the right way either. The object of contemplation is the mind itself. However, since observing the mind takes time and practice, you may find such vehicles very useful in achieving your first quantum leap into a meditative state, and it is important to note that their principal function is not religious in the sense of pledging oneself to a particular deity or religion.

Our mind is used to wandering and having random thoughts. We need some inconspicuous means to harness our attention, what the late, great nineteenth-century psychologist William James called "the essential phenomenon of will." Quite simply, when we attend to one thing and one thing only, other things take a back seat. This can be validated using neuroscience augmented by quantum physics.

Earlier in this book, I related how my own initial breakthrough in meditation came simply by counting; later, I learned how to integrate this with breath. There are endless variations on this technique, all stemming from the Vedic sacrament of *Pranayama,* the awareness and control of respiration. By merely inhaling and exhaling to a regular, rhythmic count of one-two-three-four (silently, of course), while sitting comfortably with our backs straight and our eyes closed, we begin to take command of our neural circuitry away from external influence. In the same way, silently repeating a focus word or syllable such as

"om" (rhymes with "foam") or a phrase with each exhala-
tion prepares us to go into the meditative state.

Examples of such phrases are the Sanskrit *shanti,
shanti, shanti* (peace, peace, peace) or the Eastern Orthodox Jesus Prayer ("Lord Jesus Christ, have mercy on
me"), but the Islamic *La-ilahah-illa-Llah,* a Jewish bless-
ing, or a sequence of invented syllables will serve just as
well. A focus word should be emotionally neutral (chanting the name of your sweetheart is not advised). Select a
word that comes to you naturally. Once you have chosen
a word or phrase you should stick with it; gradually you'll
become so accustomed to it that it will pop up in your
mind automatically as soon as you start to meditate. Do
not depart from it until you have slipped over the meditative threshold. How will you know when that is? Take my
word for it, you will know.

Along the way, stray thoughts of unpaid bills, appoint-
ments, appetites, and annoyances both petty and profound will rise into your mind. Let them come, observe
them as you might observe a twig carried by a river, and let
them pass away. Don't fight them, because to fight them
is to dam the river. Simply say to yourself, "Never mind,"
and gently return to your center with the help of your chosen word. That is precisely its purpose — to prevent your
mind from drifting.

Scientists like psychologist Dr. Jeffrey M. Schwartz and
physicist Henry Stapp, as well as repeated studies at
places like MIT and the National Institute of Mental Health,
have extensively documented what happens in your brain
during mindfulness meditation. Brain circuitry is quite

literally being remapped. Neurons that normally fire in response to outside stimuli are now firing in phase with your own volition. If you doubt this, there is plenty of fMRI (functional magnetic resonance imaging) and PET scan data to back it up. The prefrontal cortex and parietal lobes have taken control of the helm away from the lower brain functions. When you are able to achieve this state consistently, you are ready for quantum meditation.

A flock of seagulls will scatter as a child runs toward them, and then they will invariably reassemble a few dozen yards up the beach. When not excited into action by the mechanisms of choice, a quantum system tends naturally toward its least excited or zero-point energy state. The great British mathematician Roger Penrose is in the vanguard of those who believe that the brain's material structure enfolds a quantum state at its most unimaginably submicroscopic level. When not impinged upon by neurochemical activity in the surrounding tissue, the least excited state is preserved, and with it, our link to the *source.* Our goal now is to clear the static and allow our mind to resonate perfectly with what I referred to in the prologue of this book as God's radio signal.

The mind is most at home when it refers only to itself, to what the Vedic lexicon calls the Atman and Western mystics have called the ground of being. *Meditation is not a matter of striving, but of setting the stage for the mind to return to its most coherent, natural, and least excited state,* to, in the words of Meister Eckhart, "Get out of the way and let God be God in you." Meditation is, by the way, also the mind's most blissful state, as evidenced by the significant rise of the neurotransmitter serotonin in the brain chemistry of deep meditators. Serotonin is the same neurotransmitter that the popular anti-depressant Prozac manipulates. I feel quite sure that my friend Norman Cousins, were he still among us, would attest to the fact that both body and mind have a natural inclination to go from illness to health and from stress to bliss. The mind seeks peace; we need only provide the avenue.

If nothing seems to be happening at first, never give up, as Matangini would say. It takes a while, maybe a week or up to a month to get comfortable with meditation. How long did it take you to learn to drive? Regular practice, on a consistent schedule, makes it more automatic and much easier with each attempt. Don't be disappointed, however, if the result is not always the same: you will derive some benefit each time.

We have now reached a point where words generally fail. But because this is a book composed of words, and you have come a long way with me, I will do my best to take you home, while counseling that the final steps are yours alone. The field of endeavor I know best is laser physics, and whether by chance or providence, it has offered me a superb metaphor (perhaps a bit more than a metaphor) for the state of mind we are seeking.

Recall that a laser beam consists of a swarm of light photons marshaled into a state of coherence (technically, the wavelike properties of all the photons are in perfect phase). In this state, the individual photons give up their individuality and become a new form of light in which each acts to reinforce the others.

Before this state is reached, however, there is a gradual buildup from what laser scientists call super-radiance, seeds of coherence that sprout when the laser medium begins to self-generate coherent light. Eventually a single coherent process takes over and lasing begins (coherent light is emitted). Likewise, the mind in deep meditation reaches a crossover point where all the momentum favors a quantum leap into perfect coherence. We just need to nourish the seed of higher coherence and let it spontaneously spread by maintaining attention to what is going on in the frontal part of our brain.

Physicist Henry Stapp has investigated many examples of what is called the Quantum Zeno Effect, which was first pointed out by George Sudarshan. It is also known as the watched pot effect, whereby a given unstable quantum state (for example, some excited state of an atom) can be maintained, in effect, by paying constant attention to it. Let me reiterate so you understand just how astounding this is: It is as if we could literally keep a pot of water at the brink of boiling by looking at it. Stapp believes it may be possible to maintain quantum brain states through willed attention.

If we could see a dashboard display of what is happening in our brains as we practice meditation, we might observe the following: The gauge that meters our brain's left parietal region, where body image is formed, shows a significant decrease in activity. The boundary between our skin and the rest of the world has, mentally speaking, dissolved. The gauge monitoring our brain's right parietal function, which orients our bodies in space and time, shows a similar drop-off. We no longer occupy fixed coordinates; we are "nonlocal." Our brain's right prefrontal lobe, the seat of worry and anxiety, is idling, while our brain's left side, the locus of joy, alertness, and enthusiasm, is surging with activity.

Of course, the foregoing is something of an oversimplification, but the general picture is neurologically accurate. As you become more adept at meditation, you will come to recognize these readings, and you will know that this is the time to cease any counting or object-oriented concentration. Your sole focus will be on making a fertile place for the seed of perfect coherence to sprout and spread its roots, and, with time, it will bud and you will feel yourself blissfully expanding, dissolving, and connecting. You may weep, but they won't be tears of sorrow or stress. You will weep because you have come home.

The more you practice this technique, the longer you will be able to sustain your own Quantum Zeno Effect. A possible EEG reading may eventually show that all regions of our brains, down to the most ancient, are in phase coherence or synchrony when we are in resonance with the fundamental source of existence. The senses have become one sense; the sources of sensation have become one source. To characterize this feeling merely as "happiness" is to understate its depth, but most of us — spiritual refugees in a world that gives us a new cause for grief each day — will find ourselves quite happy even to be merely happy, and, moreover, to have found a room in our minds from which fear has fled. You have harnessed power from the coherence. There is strength in coherent laser light, and there is power in our brain's perfect coherence.

For those inclined to label such an experience as an "Eastern thing," the same PET scan studies that led to the foregoing conclusions were conducted in 2001 with a group of Franciscan nuns, and with the same results.

Meditation's documented aftereffects on physical and mental health are too numerous to catalog here, but the new science of psychoneuroimmunology, pioneered by Norman Cousins and his personal discoveries, has established not only the cited influence on blood pressure and stress hormones but an influence on the production of antibodies against disease. A study conducted with two groups of workers receiving a flu vaccine, one group meditating and the other not, found that the leftward tilt in the meditator's brain activity promoted a more beneficial response to the vaccine.

Potentially even more important for our species is meditation's link to neuroplasticity, our brain's ability to remodel itself on the fly in response to learning and experience. The brain is not a static entity but a factory of creation in which neural components such as actin filaments are being replaced at rates as frequent as every forty seconds. Neurobiologist Michael Ehlers at Duke University Medical Center infers from a recent study that "synapses are completely turning over all of their constituents multiple times a day — a stunning finding." And, from emerging information, neuroscientists estimate that the entire brain is recycled on a bi-monthly basis! Yet, remarkably, our blueprint remains ever present, and meditation's effects on that blueprint appear to make a permanent stamp on the brain, perhaps by changes in gene expression. Once meditation becomes a regular feature in our lives, the sense that we are a part of something much larger than our individual selves remains with us.

But what do we call this larger something we sense when our minds are perfectly coherent? What did the great German mystic Meister Eckhart mean when he claimed that in spiritual rapture he saw himself with the eye of his Creator? Why do the Vedic *rishis* quietly assert, from the deep well of contemplation, "I am Brahman?" Could it be that the timeless mystical experience of oneness with the *source*, an experience that transcends all faiths and cultures, is actually the closest we humans can ever come to perceiving the universe as it truly is?

I would argue that it is the universal potentiality of consciousness that we resonate with when we tap the mind's well. We access the very power behind all existence, a power which is encrypted everywhere in the foundation of space itself. It is the power of the *one source,* the order that underlies and enfolds all orders, that unifies all fields and forms, as well as consciousness, and it will not, by now, surprise you to hear my assertion that we call this *source* by its code name: God.

Acknowledgments

I wish to thank you, dear readers, for your patience in letting me share with you the thoughts so dear to me.

I owe an exceptional gratitude to my agent, Dorris Halsey, for her determined efforts in getting the book published. I greatly appreciate A. W. Hill for his tireless endeavor and outstanding literary erudition that helped me bring the manuscript to completion. I also thank Mary Strobel for using her considerable talent in checking the final manuscript.

I am very grateful for some illuminating discussions with Professors Roger Penrose, Frank Wilczek, Basil Hiley, Charles Townes, and Henry Stapp, who also touched me with their compassion and enthusiasm.

I am indebted to Roy M. Carlisle, senior editor and my editor at the Crossroad Publishing Company, for his guidance in presenting my odyssey. Tatiana Chekhova and Mariya Marchuk deserve credit for their assistance in preparing the manuscript.

Finally, I would like to acknowledge the continuing support of my lifelong friend Dr. Jagdish Sharma, the co-author of my first scientific article. My sincere appreciation also goes to another longtime friend, Doug Taylor, who studied to become a pastor but decided to anchor his faith in science; for years we met for lunch almost every Saturday to discuss the link between science and spirituality.

I am also grateful to my friends and former colleagues Dr. Abe Zarem, Dr. Donald Hicks, Dr. William Steier, Dr. Leonard Nugent, Ellis Amburn, and Ingrid Kepler May.

The generous assistance from Dr. John Jones, Rachel Greer, Jackie Andre, and John Eagleson of Crossroad Publishing Company is greatly appreciated.

About the Author

Mani Bhaumik holds a Ph.D. and an honorary D.Sc. degree for lifetime academic achievement from the Indian Institutes of Technology, and has the rare distinction of being elected a fellow by his scientific peers to both the American Physical Society and the Institute of Electrical and Electronics Engineers. He achieved international recognition and success as a coinventor of the laser technology that made LASIK eye surgery possible, and is a principal creator and developer of Cosmic Quantum Ray, a 3-D animated cartoon series that premiered on the VOOM HD Networks in 2007. He lives in Los Angeles.

A Word from the Editor

I was standing in one of the beautiful rooms of Mani's home in the hills above Los Angeles watching his gig on *Lifestyles of the Rich and Famous.* I had heard about it for months and never seen it. So he and Tatiana, his colleague in his animation project, indulged my desire to see this brief few minutes displaying Mani's former home and lifestyle. It was impressive, I must admit. While I was standing there watching the video, I felt this immense wave of gratitude sweep over me. Gratitude for Mani's graciousness and his willingness to tell his amazing story of struggle and spirituality. Gratitude for Tatiana's graciousness to me through the months — especially one time when we were behind schedule, Mani needed more time on the manuscript, and I said, "Fine, as long as I get it back on the weekend." So Tatiana flew from LA to the Bay Area on a Saturday morning to bring me the manuscript so I would have the weekend to work on it. Gratitude to Dorris, Mani's agent, who is one of the grandes dames of publishing on the West Coast and who has been incredibly gracious to me on more than one project. And gratitude, dare I say it, to God, for allowing this man to come into my life and touch my heart and stimulate my mind.

It all started when Dorris insisted, in the way that only Dorris can, that I meet this man and talk to him about doing a book. I was deferring because I couldn't imagine how to really pull this off, even though Mani's book about his life was a bestseller in India. It seemed too remote and too esoteric for the same thing to happen here. But I had not counted on the power of that first conversation in his living room. Mani is a soft-spoken man, but as I asked questions and he quietly but passionately told me about his struggle to rise out of poverty and become a scientist — and then his struggle to make sense out of a life that had become "rich and famous" — I realized that I must and would find a way to get this story told. It is a story that you cannot ignore or dismiss. It is the story of many who come to this country and make their dreams come true, but with the added twist that this man decided to make decisions that would take him on a path toward God rather than on a path to just more riches. It is a story you will not forget any time soon.

Now when I think of standing in Mani's home, I think of a man who has become an inspiration to me and a friend. I think of how we transcend our individual spiritual traditions and share in the grace that we both know we have received. And I remain eternally grateful.

Roy M. Carlisle
Senior Editor

Dr. Bhaumik and President Ronald Reagan share a photo op after a meeting.

Bill Clinton shares some thoughts with Dr. Bhaumik.

Eva Gabor and Dr. Bhaumik at a mansion party.

Dr. Bhaumik with his friend Eddie Albert.

Of Related Interest

John Polkinghorne
QUARKS, CHAOS, AND CHRISTIANITY
Questions to Science and Religion

In a crystal-clear discussion of science and religion and their logical friendship in the search for truth and understanding, Polkinghorne draws on discoveries made in atomic physics to make credible the claims of Christianity, and helps refine Christian perceptions through the knowledge that the new science brings. He discusses belief in God, chaos, evolution, miracles, and prayer, and gives an answer to the question: Can a scientist believe?

"The most stimulating theologian writing in the field today and the only person with equal expertise in theology and quantum mechanics. We have two realms of reality to deal with if we are truly going to understand the world in which we live, and John Polkinghorne is the bridge."
—*Morton Kelsey*

Paperback, 128 pages, 978-0-8245-2406-7

Support your local bookstore,
or order directly from the publisher at
www.crossroadpublishing.com

To request a catalog or inquire about quantity
orders, contact sales@crossroadpublishing.com

crossroad